BEN CAUNT

The Nottinghamshire bare-knuckle boxer who became

CHAMPION OF ENGLAND

David Fells

DEDICATION

I dedicate this book to my late father, Maurice, a keen boxing fan.

First published 2003 by David Fells

David Fells can be contacted at:

david@bencaunt.freeserve.co.uk

www.bencaunt@freeserve.co.uk

ISBN 0-9546143-0-5

Copyright David Fells 2003

Printed by Simply Print Ltd, Loughborough, 0800 731 2004

Acknowledgements

Thanks to:

Nev Caunt, my late uncle who planted the Ben Caunt seed in my head in the 1960s.

Bob Hartley, an ex boxer and a writer of boxing books who gave me the valuable present of his time, welcomed me to his home in London and pointed me in the right direction on a number of occasions.

Sue, my wife, without whose support, assistance and enthusiasm this book would not have happened.

CONTENTS

Foreword		7
Illustrations		9
Chapter 1	A brief history of pugilism	10
Chapter 2	Ben's early years (1814-1837)	20
Chapter 3	Revenge over Bendigo (1838)	29
Chapter 4	The Battle with Brassey (1839-1840)	49
Chapter 5	Ben fights Ward for the Championship (1840)	77
Chapter 6	Champion of England! (1841)	95
Chapter 7	The Champion visits America (1841-1843)	115
Chapter 8	Bendigo takes the title (1844-1850)	126
Chapter 9	The Fire at the Coach and Horses (1851)	152
Chapter 10	Family squabble with Nat Langham (1852-1861)	163
Chapter 11	Today (2003)	188
Appendix I	Ben Caunt's career ring record	192
Appendix II	Jack Broughton's Rules of 1743	193
Appendix III	London Prize Ring Rules 1838	195
Appendix IV	Transcript of the Will of Benjamin Caunt	200
Bibliography		210
Index		211

Cover picture:

Ben posing at his peak as a Prize Fighter

FOREWORD

My father, Maurice, was a keen boxing fan who would watch all the top televised boxing matches and it was he, rather than us, who decided myself and my brother John should attend the Bestwood Village (where my father worked at the colliery) Boxing Club. In retrospect, I am pleased to have experienced that albeit brief period of time actually feeling the butterflies in the pit of my stomach as I would climb through the ropes to face another youngster. It was good to have experienced the controlled boxing artistry of self defence disappear as attack took over, driven on by fear and adrenaline and then the trickle of the 'claret[1]' as it (very regularly in my case) would run freely from my nose and down to my mouth. These things I like to feel have given me the very slightest of insights into the stories that follow. Although I too have watched the big televised fights occasionally, I am not a fan of the idea of two men facing each other in the name of sport where the sole aim of that sport is to try and inflict damage upon your opponent. I did not stay long with boxing as my heroes of that time were from football rather than boxing. This book has therefore come to fruition not so much to promote the sport of boxing but rather to record a piece of Nottinghamshire history.

My mother's maiden name was Kathleen Eva Caunt and as I researched my family tree I discovered that my mother's great great grandfather was Frederick Caunt a brother to Benjamin Caunt who was the bare-knuckle boxing champion of England. As I read this I recalled how many years earlier, as a then reluctant amateur boxer at the Bestwood Village Boxing Club, I was told by my uncle Nev Caunt (my mother's brother) that I had an ancestor who was a bare-knuckle boxer. I had stored away this information without ever really knowing the facts behind the statement, but now here he was again appearing in my family tree. After a couple of years of researching 'ordinary' working people I was suddenly quite excited by the thought of a celebrity in the family.

All I knew of Ben Caunt at this stage was that although born in Newstead in Nottinghamshire he spent much of his youth, as I did, just down the road in Hucknall. In fact his grave was in the grounds of St. Mary Magdalene, in the market place in Hucknall, the same church in fact where Sue and I had married in 1973. Off I went to both the Hucknall and Nottingham

---

[1] Blood

libraries expecting to find lots of information about him but unfortunately there was next to nothing, only a few scraps of poor quality photocopies from past local newspapers.

I was so disappointed and I needed to satisfy my thirst for information about Ben Caunt that I decided to do something about it. Although my initial intentions were not necessarily to write a book, I just had a very strong desire to know more about him. My search took me to various people and places including direct descendants of Ben who still live in Hucknall and a well respected author of boxing books in London named Bob Hartley. Bob helped me enormously and pointed me in the right direction on a number of occasions. Eventually the amount of information about Ben and his fights grew considerably and I realised that for anyone else to find out about Ben Caunt they would also be faced with having to tread a similar arduous path. This book therefore, is the result of that research being a compilation of the articles discovered about the bare-knuckle fighter who caught my imagination - Ben Caunt - Champion of England.

ILLUSTRATIONS

Jack Broughton	11
James Figg	14
An example of a Prize Fight – Broome v Hannan in 1841	16
Vincent Dowling	18
Frank Dowling	19
The young Ben Caunt	22
Ben Butler – Caunt's uncle	26
Ben Caunt	30
Bendigo (William Thompson)	34
Bendigo (William Thompson)	39
Brassey (John Leechman)	50
Peter Crawley	59
Ben Caunt and Brassey	73
James Burke – The Deaf 'Un	81
Hammer Lane	83
Ben Caunt	98
Nick Ward	111
S.S. Europe in which Ben sailed to America	117
Charles Freeman	121
William Perry – The Tipton Slasher	122
Ben Caunt with the cup presented to him by his admirers	124
Squire Osbaldeston	136
Ben Caunt and Bendigo	144
Nat Langham	165
Nat Langham	170
Ben Caunt and Nat Langham	173
The parlour of the Coach and Horses	178
The death mask of Ben Caunt	187
The Salisbury	188
The Salisbury	189
Ben Caunt's grave	190

Chapter 1

A BRIEF HISTORY OF PUGILISM

Pugilism began in England early in the 18th century and lasted until around the time of the last bare-knuckle championship fight between the American champion John L. Sullivan who beat Jake Kilrain in 75 rounds near New Orleans in 1889. In 1892 Sullivan again featured in the first championship fight using gloves when he lost to James J. Corbett again in New Orleans.

James Figg, champion with the sword and at cudgelling[2] is acknowledged as the first champion of the English Prize Ring. In 1720 he opened a school of arms in London on the Oxford Road (now Oxford Street) known as Figg's Amphitheatre. Before this, pugilism had been an occasional entertainment of fairs and a few outdoor 'rings', which as the name suggests were circular. Figg's amphitheatre was a cross between a large fairground booth and a theatre and was meant for instruction as well as exhibitions and its prices kept it exclusive. To see a contest featuring Figg himself the admission charge would be 2s 6d (12½p) which was virtually a day's wage for most workers and very expensive when compared with the usual 2d or 3d to watch a day's cricket. The contests and coaching were not exclusively boxing but also between swordsmen and quarterstaff specialists. One of the best fist-fighters to appear at the amphitheatre was Jack Broughton.

Upon Figg's death in 1734 George Taylor took over the management of the amphitheatre. Taylor called himself champion, an impertinence when everyone knew that Jack Broughton had never been beaten by anybody and the list of his victims included George Taylor. Broughton began to find his supportive role more and more frustrating and was keen for his independence. By now he was a popular man with a growing circle of influential friends and his ideas for an amphitheatre devoted wholly to fisticuffs fell on receptive ears, particularly as he promised much better facilities for spectators than Taylor's emporium offered. Broughton's amphitheatre opened on Taylor's doorstep on 13th March 1743. Everyone, except for George Taylor, was happy with Broughton's new theatre, with its boxes and gallery for those seeking space and comfort and its pit for those who crowded round the raised stage. After a series of fights which clashed with and undercut (maximum

---

[2] Fighting with short heavy sticks.

Jack Broughton

price of 1s 6d) Taylor succumbed, closing his own theatre and took his fighters to join Broughton.

Jack Broughton decided he needed a set of rules to assist in the smooth running of the contests in his amphitheatre. In the same way as the Jockey Club saw itself regulating Newmarket racing only, 'Jack Broughton's Rules' (see Appendix II) as they became known, were not formulated as national rules for pugilism but they were destined to govern prize-fighting for almost a century.

This new sport became popular and fights for money stakes (or prize-fights) drew big crowds, although they were against the law. Men were carefully trained to meet in the roped-off 'ring', usually marked out in a field. Fights went to a finish, that is, until one of the pair was unable to continue. A round ended when one of the boxers fell to the ground, whether after many minutes, or after only a few seconds. When a round ended, the seconds took their men to their corners and attended them during an interval of half a minute. After this pause, the boxers again came 'to the scratch' and set to. If either failed to stand up after thirty seconds the fight was over, the loser said to be 'knocked out of time' or 'not up to scratch'. Some prize-fights lasted for hours; others ended in a few minutes.

Boxing with bare knuckles was a matter of straight hitting with both right and left, while foot movements were not as free as they are in modern boxing. Turf was underfoot and it was usual to wear shoes with spikes or studs. The men stood close and were allowed to grapple and throw one another to the ground.

Training for these battles is best described by Pierce Egan in his Boxiana when he describes Captain Barclay's recommendations for bringing athletes to a state of competitive perfection:

"The skilful trainer attends to the state of the bowels, the lungs and the skin; and he uses such means as will reduce the fat and, at the same time, invigorate the muscular fibres. The patient is purged by drastic medicines; he is sweated by walking under a load of clothes and by lying between feather beds. His limbs are roughly rubbed. His diet is beef or mutton; his drink, strong ale; and he is gradually inured to exercise.... [He] enters upon his training with a regular course of physic, which consists of three doses. Glauber Salts are generally preferred; and from one ounce and a half to two ounces are taken each time, with an interval of four days between each dose. After having gone through the course of physic, he commences his regular exercise.... He must rise at five in the morning, run half a mile at top speed uphill and walk six miles at a moderate pace, coming in about seven to breakfast, which should consist of beef-steaks or mutton-chops under-done, with stale bread and old beer. After breakfast, he must again walk six miles at a moderate pace and at twelve lie down in bed without his clothes for half an hour. On getting up, he must walk four miles and return by four to dinner, which should also be beef steaks or mutton chops, with bread and beer as at breakfast. Immediately after dinner, he must resume his exercise, by running half a mile at the top of his speed and walking six miles at a moderate pace. He takes no more exercise for that day....

After having gone on in this regular course for three or four weeks, he must take a four-mile sweat, which is produced by running four miles, in flannel, at the top of his speed. Immediately on returning, a hot liquor is prescribed. It is termed the sweating liquor and is composed of the following ingredients, viz. one ounce of caraway-seed; half an ounce of coriander-seed; one ounce of root liquorice; and half an ounce of sugar-candy; mixed with two bottles of cider and boiled down to one-half. He is then put to bed in his flannels and being covered with six or eight pairs of blankets and a feather-bed, must remain in this state from twenty-five to thirty minutes, when he is taken out and rubbed perfectly dry. Being then well wrapped in his great coat he walks out gently for two miles and returns to break-fast, which, on such occasions, should consist of a roasted fowl. He afterwards proceeds with his usual exercise. These sweats are continued weekly. If the stomach be foul, an emetic or two must be given, about a week before the conclusion of the training and he is now supposed to be in the highest condition.

Besides his usual or regular exercise, a person under training ought to employ himself in the intervals in every kind of exertion, which tends to activity, such as cricket, bowls, throwing quoits, &c. so that, during the whole day, both body and mind may be constantly occupied."

Captain Barclay was a firm believer in meat as the best training food. He permitted no vegetables to be eaten 'as they are watery and of difficult digestion.' Butter and cheese were forbidden, 'the one being very indigestible and the other apt to turn rancid on the stomach.' Only the yolks of eggs (raw in the morning) were given a place on the training table and milk was condemned 'as it curdles on the stomach.' Soups and other warm fluids were outlawed. The trainee had discretion in only one matter: of the foods allowed, he could eat as much or as little as his appetite dictated.

Pugilism had a major influence on artists, poets and writers of the day with possibly cricket being the only sport to receive a greater coverage.

The painters Hogarth and Moreland were on friendly terms with prize-fighters whilst the caricaturists Rowlandson and Gillray were often to be seen at ringside. Prize-fighting was described and Prize Ring jargon used by many of the leading literary figures of the time, writers as respected and respectable as Fielding, Dickens and Thackeray with Lord Byron revelling in the company of pugilists. Pugilism also produced writers like Pierce Egan and Vincent Dowling, who spent the greater part of their working lives specifically chronicling the events of the Prize Ring and the character of its protagonists. At the same time, literally tons of cheap prints and broadsheets were produced, depicting the latest heroes and most important fights, for the consumption of the illiterate or semi literate masses.

An admiring public presented the leading fighters with ornate championship belts, silver cups and services of plate. Eulogised and feted by the literati and worshipped by the mob during their lifetime, in death they were commemorated with splendid tombs.

At the height of the craze for pugilism, the popular Blackwood's Magazine had remarked, albeit tongue in cheek, that the man who has not read Boxiana is ignorant of the power of the English language. Moreover, prize-fighting as a popular spectacle was responsible for the introduction into our native tongue not just of slang words like claret, meaning blood, but also of many metaphors still in common use. 'The phrases 'throw your hat into the ring', 'come up to scratch' and 'throw in the sponge', are all echoes of archaic Prize Ring practice.

Pugilistic lore is preserved in the riotous antics of the cartoon characters Tom and Jerry who were originally portrayed in human form as a pair of unruly Regency bucks, the invention of fight reporter Pierce Egan.

In 1838 a new set of rules were introduced to replace Jack Broughton's Rules and these were known as the Rules of the London Prize Ring or The New Rules.

James Figg

The New Rules of 1838 were an attempt, one of several, to bring a greater order and acceptability to the sport. They coincided with the death of 'Brighton Bill' in a fight with Owen Swift, a much publicised tragedy which resulted in the Home Office adding its pressures to those of the reformers by way of urging local authorities to put down prize-fighting. The claim made for the New Rules was that they were 'more manly and humane'. What they resulted in, in practice, was greatly increased scope for dispute and disagreement. Whereas Broughton's rules, in so far as they were concerned with ring practice and not with gambling, had confined themselves to a simple protection against foul blows and being struck when down, the new code tried to cover all eventualities, from the length of the spikes in a fighter's shoes to the prohibition 'of hard substances, such as stones or sticks, or a resin in the hand during the battle'. Fouls included not only falling without a blow (although a man was allowed to slip down in a maul to avoid punishment), but also butting, kneeing and hugging against the ropes. Once a boxer's knee was on the ground, whether at close quarters or at a distance, he was 'down' and this gave legitimacy to what became almost the standard fashion of ending fights - going down quickly on the knee to tempt an opponent into a foul blow, or for a beaten man, deliberately hitting a crouching man as a less painful and less decisive way of accepting defeat. Broughton's two umpires remained, but whereas he had seen them as appealing to a third party only in the case of disagreement, the New Rules accepted the inevitability of dispute and prescribed a referee, confining his role though, to settling matters referred to him by the umpires. With fight crowds becoming less and less restrained, the rules of combat becoming more legalistic and fighters and their promoters becoming ever more devious, the role of referee became an increasingly thankless one and few took it upon themselves with anything but the most real reluctance.

Challenges from fighters, details of forthcoming fights and reports of recent contests were all broadcast by the sporting press of the time. The number one sporting newspaper was Bell's Life in London and was the forerunner of today's Sporting Life.

Bell's Life in London did not only report the sporting news but it also promoted the sports it covered, both creating and feeding the interest. The editor at the time was George Vincent Dowling who was convinced about his paper's influence, claiming that it was responsible for the popularity of cricket and for its spread over the country. The newspaper also covered

*An example of a prize fight –
Broome v Hannan in 1841*

boxing comprehensively with Dowling himself and later Henry Downes Miles personally attending the fights and reporting the round by round details, with as many as 3000 words covering the major fights.

It can be seen from venues that appeared in the newspaper that there was a move away from the London area so that by the 1840's over half of all fights had moved to the Midlands and North of the country.

Bell's Life in London not only reported the fights, it also provided the publicity which fed and fostered interest in the Prize Ring throughout the country and during the peak years it provided some of those organisational elements which helped pugilism to survive. The editor became the regular holder of the stake money for pugilism and other sports, at times holding as much as £15,000 and his journalistic colleagues were regularly called upon to referee sporting events.

Towards the end of the 19th century this connection was finally broken and although the editor was still holding the stake-money he had forbidden any of his staff from officiating at prize-fights, following several painful episodes of attacks from disaffected spectators.

Soon after 1870 the 'Ring' section of the newspaper was reduced considerably. The fight reports had once spread generously over one of the massive pink pages and at its peak (around the middle of the 19th century) recorded over 150 fights each year. It had now been reduced to the occasional brief sub-paragraph under the heading of 'Boxing and Wrestling' and this was in an even thicker newspaper, which was giving virtually full page coverage to such sports as angling and billiards.

When gloves were adopted for contests (after earlier being used in training), hooking, swinging and upper cutting were brought into play. Faster and more varied footwork came into use with the springy surface of the modern ring.

Later in the 19th century the Prize Ring lost the fashionable supporters who had encouraged it in the time of the Napoleonic wars and it fell on bad days. Yet even in 1860 the fight at Farnborough between the English champion, Tom Sayers and John C. Heenan of America, was watched by a large crowd and fully reported in English and American newspapers.

As boxing became less brutal, mainly because of the rules drawn up in 1867 by the 8th Marquess of Queensbury, which insisted on such things as padded gloves being worn and other changes to ensure fair play it eventually came to be permitted by law.

Finally, just a couple of points to bear in mind when reading this book. Firstly, the average height of the British male has increased since the middle of the nineteenth century so a well-proportioned man of six feet two and a half inches in those days would have been even more impressive than he would today. Secondly, the often fought for stake of one hundred pounds would be worth about five thousand pounds today – so a figure many people would consider well worth fighting for!

Vincent Dowling – The Editor of Bell's Life for thirty years

Frank Dowling – Took over as editor of Bell's Life from his father Vincent in 1851

Chapter 2

BEN'S EARLY YEARS

(1814-1837)

Ben Caunt was born in a little cottage east of Newstead railway station a few miles from Hucknall Torkard (hereafter referred to as Hucknall as it is now called) in Nottinghamshire on the 22nd March 1814. The Nottinghamshire records showing that his christening took place at Hucknall's St. Mary Magdalene's Church on 15th May 1814, although most records refer to him being born in 1815. His parents Robert and Martha (nee Butler) were married at the same church on the 1st of November 1802 and had five sons with the records showing the following christenings (as births were not officially recorded in England until 1837): William (24/7/1803), Frederick (31/3/1805), Cornelius (27/9/1807), Benjamin (15/5/1814) and Robert (6/8/1821).

Ben's parents were tenants of Lord Byron the poet, a fact that Ben, in later years, was fond of recounting. His father was employed in some humble capacity on the Newstead Abbey estate and according to Ben his own earliest employment was as a game-keeper on the Newstead estate although it was more likely that he was in fact a labourer, a role for which he would have been very well suited as, before he was 21 years old he weighed 14st 7lbs and stood 6ft 2½ins tall.

He appears at an early age to have aspired to pugilistic honours and soon acquired a reputation amongst the other local youngsters. He was brought up in a fighting atmosphere, for pitched battles used to be fought by the youths of Hucknall, one group at the 'Buildings' and the other lot in the town, with one set calling themselves 'Boney's men' and the others 'Wellington's' after the famous rival commanders, with Ben being one of these spirited lads. Another side of his career; though a short one no doubt, was that when the Baptists rented a house in Red Lion Yard he acted as candle-snuffer.

Ben took part in both wrestling and boxing with the other local youths and was soon the pick of the bunch. On the village green, at wrestling, there was not a lad could throw him and with the gloves he held his own against all comers. With the fists too, he had proved himself no mean performer and had started by thrashing two big fellows, older than himself, who had ventured to tackle the young giant. Ben fought a number of minor and unrecorded fights before embarking on his Prize Ring career. These fights included a relative, Richard Butler at Wighay Field in Hucknall and George Graham of Lincolnshire, both of which he won.

At the same time in Nottingham, William Thompson, better known as Bendigo, was also taking on and beating the local boxing talent and was building himself quite a reputation within the Nottingham area.

About the time that Bendigo was being taken great notice of at Nottingham, in 1834, young Caunt was but nineteen years of age and very little known outside his native village. But there was one Jack Ridsdale who lived at Hucknall and took great notice of the young giant, predicting that he would, if properly taken in hand, turn out to be a top class fighter. A great friend of Mr. Ridsdale was Mr. Joseph Whitaker, of Ramsdale House, near Nottingham Forest and one of the most eccentric gentlemen throughout the Midlands. He was known as The Duke of Limbs. One who was well acquainted with him thus describes him: "Joe Whitaker was one of the finest specimens of the old breed of English yeomen we have ever come across. A giant in strength and constitution was Joe, with a fine, open handsome English face, adorned with a pair of huge whiskers, clipped till they looked like a great hair brush on each cheek. But the limbs of the man were the most astonishing part of him, none of your blubber and truffles, but literally all muscle and bone, with a figure-head and an out-water in happy keeping with the goodly hull". Hence Joe's sobriquet, 'His Grace of Limbs.'

No better sportsman or more convivial bon vivant ever breathed - the prince of hosts, his home was the model of a hospitable English homestead. But he was eccentric - too fond of practical jokes to be altogether an agreeable acquaintance to commonplace folks. He was a keen and passionate lover of the Prize Ring. It was only natural then, that a man of this class should recognise the talents of Bendigo and indeed, from the very first he took a fancy to the young Nottingham pugilist, who was as eccentric as himself and determined to match him as soon as the opportunity occurred.

He had not long to wait, for, being on a visit to his friend Ridsdale, Joe Whitaker was taken to see a wrestling match in the village, one of the competitors being young Caunt and the other a man from Lincolnshire named Potter. Ben came off an easy winner and Mr. Whitaker was struck with the youngster's mighty limbs. So when his friend launched out into praises of Caunt's courage and skill as a boxer, he thought to himself there would be a

The young Ben Caunt

fine opportunity of matching Master Bendigo. A few weeks after the wrestling match, Joe Whitaker once more paid a visit to Hucknall, but this time accompanied by Bendigo and a set of gloves, suggesting to Mr. Ridsdale that the two lads should have the gloves on. This was readily agreed to and young Caunt was sent for and in the garden the two men, who were destined to make such names and climb to the top of the tree met for the first time in their lives. It was a complete contrast in style with Bendigo quick and agile and Ben slower and more ponderous but with the greater strength. Both Caunt and his backer were exceedingly pleased at the trial and readily took up the challenge thrown down by Bendigo to fight in the twenty-four foot ring for £25 a side.

That same evening Joe Whitaker and Bendigo walked into Mr. Jephson's, the Lion and Unicorn, Newcastle Street, Nottingham and announced that the match was made, much to the delight of several sports who had foregathered there and who were all willing to have an interest in the battle-money, so that really, Mr. Whitaker had only to find the training expenses; which would easily be covered by a tenner.

The date fixed for the battle was Tuesday, July 21st, 1835 and the place selected was Appleby House on the Ashbourne Road, thirty miles from Nottingham and twenty-two from Birmingham. Sam Turner took Bendigo under his wing and trained him at the Green Dragon, Chilwell, just outside Nottingham, whilst Ben Butler, Caunt's uncle, looked after his nephew. Although neither of the men were as yet 'famous' there was by all accounts a fair muster at Appleby House which was a well known roadside inn where cocking and other sports went on and where, in the large meadow at the back many a fight had been brought off. It was in this field five years previous to the battle that is about to be described, that Harry Preston of Birmingham beat Dick Hill of Nottingham and old Jack Powell, or 'Sir John' as he was dubbed, the landlord of the house, declared that he had never taken so much money in the house in his life. It was upon that occasion even Mr. Dowson, the lord of the manor and a magistrate, witnessed the contest seated on his cob[3] and made not the slightest attempt to interfere.

Many came from Birmingham and the Nottingham district and amongst those present were: Mr. Beardsworth, Mr. Ridsdale and, of course, Joe Whitaker, Arthur Matthewson (who was selected as referee), Jack Matthews, Philip Bryant Sampson and Harry Potter, the stylish commissary of the Midlands.

---

[3] A stocky short legged horse.

Harry was well known for his marvellous get-up - white hat cocked on one side, extraordinary waistcoats and enormous seals hanging from his watch-chain. Caunt was waited upon by his uncle, Ben Butler and Harry Bamford, whilst his father was also close to his corner, anxious no doubt as to the result of the young hopeful's first important appearance in the Prize Ring. Bendigo had his seconds Sam Turner (his trainer) and Sam Merryman, the well-known lightweight. Caunt was in his twenty-first year and he was certainly the biggest man who had thrown his castor[4] into the arena since Tom Brown, of Bridgnorth.

There was of course, a great disparity in their sizes and Bendy must have looked quite David beside this Goliath, yet the smaller man had better figure for an athlete, Caunt had no symmetry or grace about his figure - big bones, prominent muscles and tremendous limbs. His opponent was a powerfully built man and possessed of great strength, well proportioned springy, sinewy and muscular, with a combination of power and agility.

Bendigo fought with his right foot foremost, a puzzling attitude for a man who has been accustomed to spar in the usual left-legged manner, but he could change quickly when necessary. Caunt stood in a clumsy attitude and indeed, never through his fighting career could ever be taught to stand otherwise. Bendigo eyed his adversary quite coolly and confidently no doubt due to the way he felt things had gone at that little boxing bout they had had together in the garden. Here is an account of the start of the battle:

'Erect and square towered the massive figure of Big Ben but Bendy dropped his right shoulder and stooped a little, as if meditating a spring. The question was, who should begin? This Ben speedily settled by bearing down like a huge three decker, with all sails set, onto his foe. Bendy drew back, Ben pressed on anxious to get his sledgehammer fist home somewhere on the other's carcass. Smack at last went his right half-round at the head. Bendy ducked and before the Big 'Un could realise what he was about, the lithe Nottingham man sprang in and nailed Caunt a tremendous blow on the nose. Ben stopped short and put up his hand to the wounded organ, amid mingled cheers from the crowd. A second later the blood came slowly trickling from the giant's nostrils and a roar of 'First blood to Bendy ' proclaimed that the premier event had been booked to Mr. William Thompson. Caunt shook his head and went gamely for his man again - another sweeping right-hander;

---

[4] A hat

missed clean and, quick as lightning, Bendy nailed him again on the nose and was away before the Big 'Un could touch him.

This was not at all what Caunt had expected as nothing of that sort had happened in the garden with the gloves and he was puzzled. Caunt, losing his temper, dashed after Bendy, in order to give him one of his hugs, but the wily one slipped down just as Ben was about to grip and sat on the turf grinning at his opponent, much to the disgust of Ben, who walked angrily to his corner.

And so the fight proceeded - round after round there is repetition, Bendigo being too quick for his man and planting blow after blow upon the bruised and bleeding face of the countryman. Bendy always avoided the clumsy and slow returns by dropping. Ben was becoming maddened with pain and still more by the exasperating tactics of his adversary, who escaped a hiding every time by going down. At the close of the twenty-second round Caunt lost all control over himself. In a blind fury he rushed across the ring to Bendy's corner before the watch-holder had called "Time" and whilst his opponent was still sitting on Turner's knee. "Wilt thou stand up and foight fair thou damned hound?" spluttered out Ben in his passion - but before Bendy could answer, the giant lifted his arm and with a tremendous hander sent both Bendy and Sam Turner rolling on the turf. "Foul", "Foul", was the cry from Bendigo's friends; and as the blow had been deliberately struck, the two umpires and referee were unanimously of the opinion that Caunt had by this outrageous act of folly lost the fight.'

It was a very unsatisfactory affair, but it showed that Bendigo was an exceedingly artful tactician and when it became known that the little one had stood up to their giant and given him dreadful punishment the Nottingham man became at once celebrated. Whilst Caunt had proved himself to be as brave as a lion and ready and willing to go on receiving any amount of punishment.

The following report appeared in the press at the time:

A fight took place in the Nottingham district between two youngsters who were both fated to develop into Champions of England. The meeting place was near Appleby House, on the Ashbourne Road, about thirty miles from Nottingham. Both men were natives of Nottinghamshire; the elder one,

Ben Butler – Caunt's uncle

William Thompson, hailing from the county town, while the younger, Benjamin Caunt, was a native of the village of Hucknall, where his parents had been tenants of the poet Lord Byron, a fact of which the athlete was always intensely proud. Caunt on this occasion made his first appearance in any ring and having been born on the 22nd of March 1814 had only just completed his twenty-first year and had therefore a very considerable disadvantage in point of age. On the other hand, he was a youngster of Herculean proportions and giant strength; stood 6ft. 2in in height and his fighting weight was 14st. 7lb. Thus, in point of size, it was a horse to a hen; but Caunt had no science at all, while Bendigo had a very considerable share of it. The Big 'Un was seconded by Ben Butler and Bamford and Bendigo by Turner and Merryman.

Throughout twenty-two rounds Caunt stood up with indomitable pluck and perseverance to receive a long way the lion's share of the punishment, while his shifty opponent always avoided the return by getting down. Caunt at last, in a rage at these tactics, which he could not counteract or endure, rushed across the ring, called on him to stand up, before the call of "Time" by the umpires and then struck Bendigo before he rose from his second's knee. The referee and umpires having decided that this blow was foul, the stakes; £25 a side, were awarded to Bendigo. It was the expressed opinion of the spectators that, had Caunt kept his temper and husbanded his strength, the issue would have gone the other way, as he proved himself game to the backbone, while his opponent was made up of dodges from heel to headpiece.

This fight had the effect of calling the attention of backers to both men. Of Bendigo's cleverness there could be no question and Caunt's enormous strength and unflinching courage were equally indisputable. It may be fair to say that the pugilistic careers of both these men commenced with this fight when they were, of course, standing at the bottom of the ladder. Unbeknown to them they would meet again when they were halfway up the ladder and a third time when they both stood on the topmost rung.

This victory over the gigantic wrestler of Hucknall could not fail to bring his conqueror prominently before the eyes of the boxing world. John Leechman, (more commonly known as Brassey of Bradford), Charley Langham, Looney of Liverpool, Bob Hampson, also of Liverpool indeed, all the big 'uns of the prize-fighting fraternity were anxious to have a shy at the audacious 11st 10lb man who had beaten Ben the Giant.

According to the stories of Bendigo he was one of triplets, nicknamed Shadrach, Meshach and Abednego after the three young men thrown into the 'fiery furnace' on the orders of King Nebuchadnezzar. However, the parish register of Saint Mary's Church records that Richard and William, twin sons of Mr. and Mrs. Thompson were baptised on 16th October, 1811. Perhaps the third baby died soon after birth, for little William Thompson was always called 'Bendy' and it therefore seems likely that he was originally one of three. Nobody ever called him William and at the start of his career in the Prize Ring he fought as Abednego Thompson. This was later shortened to Bednego and then changed again to Bendigo.

Another theory as to how he came to have the name Bendigo was given in Bell's Life after the account of the second meeting between the two Nottinghamshire opponents, which stated that he acquired the name from his style of boxing. He would always approach his opponent bent over and as soon as he had managed to land a blow he would then move away to avoid any retaliation and hence 'Bend and go' was his style, later changed to Bendigo. As to which theory is correct is open to conjecture, but both are interesting possibilities.

Caunt did not fight again during the next two years preferring to prepare and train now he had experience and a good understanding of the kind of skills required in the Prize Ring. He may, of course, have taken part in low key 'warm up' bouts not recorded by the press. Caunt's next two 'official' fights were not recorded in detail in the Prize Ring reports in Bell's Life. The first of these two was on the 17th of August 1837 where he met and defeated a local celebrity, William Butler, at Stoneyford, Notts, in fourteen rounds, for a stake of £20 a side. Butler weighed around 12 stone and was beaten by weight, strength and determination, though in true Caunt fashion with very little scientific fighting. Later in November of the same year Caunt met Boneford for £25 a side and polished him off in only six rounds at Sunrise Hill, Notts.

Neither of these two opponents had previously achieved very much of note in the Prize Ring but both proved tough competitors and consequently Caunt made many friends over the affairs. It was in fact these same friends who felt he had improved to such an extent that he should tackle his original opponent Bendigo once again and attempt to revenge his earlier defeat.

Chapter 3

REVENGE AGAINST BENDIGO

(1838)

Almost three years had passed since the two Nottinghamshire rivals had met and during that period Ben had fought twice while Bendigo had fought three times.

Bendigo defeated Brassey of Bradford on May 24th 1836 for £25 a side, followed by Young Langan of Liverpool on January 24th 1837 also for £25 a side and finally Bill Looney on June 13th 1837 for £100 a side.

Their first battle proved two things distinctly, that Bendigo was one of the trickiest, most artful and quickest pugilists in the Prize Ring and that Caunt, if a bit slow, had enormous strength and unflinching courage.

A problem with the two men meeting again was the asking price as Bendigo had raised his fee and would not now consider a match for less than £100 a side. As he was dependant upon his earnings from boxing, whether fighting, teaching, or carrying out exhibitions he was now famous enough to warrant him sticking to his price.

After his three victories over Brassey, Langan and Looney, Bendigo was taken in hand by Jem Ward the ex champion who announced his intention to match Bendigo with Deaf Burke the current champion as soon as he returned from America. Meanwhile, opponents were trying to get Bendigo to agree to fight for less than the £100 he was insisting upon. Bill Looney did all he knew to induce the Nottingham man to fight him for less and Tom Britten, of Liverpool tried repeatedly to get the fight on for £50 a side, but to no avail. Bendigo stuck out for the century and he publicly announced that it was a waste of time for anybody to challenge him for less.

These explcits could not fail to attract public attention and the patrons of the Prize Ring were anxious to bring the antagonists together once again, an anxiety fully shared by Caunt and Bendigo themselves.

Ben Caunt

Two of Caunt's friends, a Mr Braithwaite and a Captain Hemyng, who believed implicitly in the powers of the Hucknall giant, resolved to back him to give him the chance to turn the tables on Bendigo.

Caunt had never been satisfied with the result of the first meeting saying that but for the shifty tactics of Bendigo he would have won easily and openly stated that given the chance, he would thrash Mr William Thompson on their second meeting.

With the £100 found for him by his two patrons, the match was made to come off 'at Sheffield or 100 miles thereof' but was later narrowed down to the neighbourhood of Doncaster, with the date being fixed for April 3rd, 1838. The venue in these circumstances was always vague in order to try and avoid the unwelcome attendance of the police and magistrates. The specific details of the place of the fight was announced and passed on by word of mouth much nearer the actual time, usually on the day of the fight.

Bendigo went to train under Peter Taylor at Liverpool where he was a big favourite and he made good progress. Meanwhile Caunt was being vigorously worked by his uncle, Ben Butler and later by Young Molyneaux (James Wharton), at Appleby in Leicestershire.

As it was not possible to officially announce the venue of the fight the word was spread around as far afield as London, Liverpool, Manchester, Birmingham, Sheffield and Nottingham that if anyone interested in the fight were to make their way to Doncaster they would find themselves 'on the spot' for the important business on hand.

A number of people, including the representatives of Bell's Life caught the Glasgow Mail stagecoach starting from the Bull and Mouth Aldersgate Street in London on the morning of April 2nd. After a long drive on a very cheerless day they arrived in Doncaster and put up at the Salutation or Angel Inn, as they were the famous coaching and sporting public houses of the day in the Doncaster area.

A report of the journey undertaken and recorded by the representatives of Bell's Life in London went as follows:

'At Sheffield, or within 100 miles thereof,' was the mysterious fixture for the big tourney, on Saturday evening, at half-past seven, we threw ourselves into the Glasgow mail, on our route to Doncaster, between which town and Selby we had been informed the affair was to be decided. Adventures in stage-coaches have often afforded topics for amusing detail; but we confess, from the laborious duties which fall to our lot to perform, private as well as public, every week of our lives, the last day, or rather the last night, of the week is not the one we should select as that most propitious to collect materials (if such materials were wanting) for filling a column in our ensuing publication.

In taking our place in the mail, therefore, we looked forward rather to the enjoyment of an occasional snooze than to the hope that we should discover any subject on which to dilate at a future period, where as to the character of our fellow-travellers, the general appointments of the drag or the peculiarities of the coachmen or guards - of the former we had four and the latter two, in the course of the journey - and these we will at once dismiss, by stating, at the outset, that they did their duty admirably - taking care, as 'in duty bound', to seek the usual mark of approbation by farewell hints in the common-place terms of "I leave you here, gentlemen" - in other words, 'tip' and 'go' - a laconic mode of address which by all travellers is well understood, however coolly appreciated when spoken at an open door on a cold frosty night, as the night of Saturday was and at a moment when you may perhaps have been dreaming of the 'joys you left behind you'. Quietness and repose being our first study, we soon placed our hat in the suspending-straps at the top of the rail and our travelling-cap over head and then, quietly reclining in the corner with our back to the horses, waited for the start from the yard of the Bull and Mouth. We found one old gentleman had taken his seat before us, who subsequently followed our example in taking the same side of the coach with ourselves and was not less careful in guarding himself against the chilling influence of a hard frost. A third gentleman soon after joined us and we were whirled round to the Post Office, St. Martin's-le-Grand, whence we shortly commenced our journey at a slapping pace. On reaching Islington, a fourth passenger, of colossal size, filled up the vacant seat. Few words, if any, were spoken; and the only interruption to the monotony of the night's travel was the frequent popping out and in of the last-mentioned gentleman to comfort his 'inward man' with drops of brandy with which he so perfumed our leathern convenience on his return that if we were as sensitive as some Frenchman of whom we have heard (who dined upon the effluvia of the good things he could not otherwise enjoy) we should certainly has been pretty jolly before he took his leave of us at peep of day. His departure gave occasion for the first indication that our companions were gifted with the power of speech.

Their words were few and these only had reference to the 'spirited' propensities of the gentleman who had just vacated his seat. On this there could be no difference of opinion and consequently no argument- so that we soon relapsed into the appearance at least of sleep, which was maintained with great perseverance till a brilliant sun shining through the ice-covered windows called forth a remark on the fineness of the morning. This, to our surprise, for we thought ourselves incognito, was followed by a remark of recognition from the third gentleman who had entered the coach at the Bull and Mouth and who, alluding to quick travelling, recalled to our mind some feats of this sort in which we had been engaged in the course of a twenty years' connection with the Press. The ice once broken, conversation commenced, with apparent satisfaction to us all, the venerable gentleman on my right joining and contributing as well as exacting his proportion of information on all manner of topics - public men and public measures and the public Press, forming prominent subjects of remark, upon all of which our friend on the right seemed agreeably conversant. We soon discovered that our opposite neighbour was going to Leeds, to and from which town he was a frequent traveller; but respecting the other we could form no opinion. Regarding ourselves, our secret had been divulged and we stood forward and confessed we were representatives of Bell's Life in London.

Sporting of various descriptions opened new sources of gossip and here we found 'the unknown' as much at home as ourselves. It came out, in fact, that he had been a breeder of racehorses and a patron of the Turf for pleasure, but not for profit - that he had been steward at Newmarket and that, in fact, he knew all the leading Turfites of the age and was familiar with all the recent important events on the Turf.

All this lead us to surmise that he was 'somebody', but who, we confess, we did not attempt to speculate. We found him a most pleasant associate and with that we were content. Upon the subject of our own trip to Doncaster we were silent, for we considered that was 'nothing to nobody'. The Ring as connected with our British sports was but slightly alluded to - and against the objections that were made arising out of the late fatal issue of the combat between Swift and Brighton Bill, we argued it was a casualty purely the result of an accident, which might have occurred on any other athletic competition in which no personal animosity existed and wound up by saying that there was one unanswerable argument even to the opponents of prize-fighting, that as by

William Thompson - Bendigo

them the principals were invariably considered worthless and deserving of punishment, in becoming the instrument of punishing each other, they were only fulfilling the ends of justice, without the necessity of legal interference. We referred, of course, to the recent painful exhibition of the frequent use of the knife and the strong remarks which the increasing extent of this treacherous mode of revenge had called from the judges; but upon these points our unknown friend, as we take the liberty of calling him, did not seem disposed to break a lance and subject dropped. At last we reached Grantham, where our fellow travellers forewarned us we should have an excellent breakfast and certainly one served in better taste or in greater profusion we never enjoyed. Here we met in the same room the Quaker member for Durham (Mr Pease), on his way to the north, between whom and the 'Unknown' there was a friendly recognition, but we still made no effort to lift the veil by which he was enshrouded.

On again taking our seats in the mail, we were alone with the old gentleman, our Leeds friend having mounted the roof, so that we had it all to ourselves. The chat was as pleasant to us as before - new topics were broached, the description of the localities through which we passed - the 'Dukery' (a sort of concentration of ducal seats), - afforded us both amusement and information. Now, for the first time, when conversation flagged, on watching the physiognomy of the 'Unknown', we imagined there was a meaning smile on his countenance, which seemed to say "This fellow does not know to whom he is talking" and we confess we began to try back and see where we had said anything to which exception could be taken; and more especially whether anything had dropped from us whence the intent of our journey could be collected; for we began to suspect we had been talking to a beak, who was going down expressly to spoil sport and who was chuckling within himself at the disappointment we were sure to incur. But all was safe - we had kept our secret and from anything that has dropped from us everything was as 'right as day'; indeed we dismissed the thought of treachery from our mind and we are now glad we did so, for it would have been most unjustly adopted; for although a beak of the first magnitude was in truth before us, we are persuaded he had no sinister feeling towards us or the sport we anticipated. But we have spun our yarn longer than we had intended and will come to the denouement at once. We now rattled into the clean and quiet town of Doncaster with the customary flourish of the horn and reached the Angel safe and sound. As we had collected that our companion was going no further, we were satisfied our doubts as to his real character would soon be removed; they were, sooner than we expected; for scarcely had he stepped forth when "My Lord!" was congratulated on his safe arrival.

My lord! thought we and following his example, our first effort on stretching our cramped limbs was by a respectful touch of our tile to acknowledge the honour we had enjoyed - an honour, by-the-bye, which confirmed us in the good old maxim, 'Where ignorance is bliss 'tis folly to be wise'. An answer to a simple question soon put us in possession of the 'great secret'. It was to a noble Baron who was about to preside at the Pontefract sessions we were indebted for a pleasing relief to a tedious journey; and while we acknowledge his lordship's kindness and urbanity, permit us to add that there was not a sentiment uttered by him in our presence to which we do not heartily respond. We are sure it will be gratifying to our milling readers to hear that although the fight which has given occasion for this episode was announced to take place in the district of Pontefract, formerly represented by a milling member (John Gully Esq., of Ackworth Hall. Elected M.P. for Pontefract 1832) neither our noble companion nor any of his sessional coadjutors offered any interference.

By Monday evening the town of Doncaster was very lively. So much so that it was difficult to find anywhere to sleep as the inns of the town and on the roads leading to the town, were filled to overflowing and however quiet it was in the surrounding towns, Doncaster was all bustle and commotion.

In order to avoid the hustle and bustle of the town Bendigo stayed at the White Swan at Askerne - a pretty little village about seven miles out of Doncaster on the Selby Road, famous for its sulphurous spring. The spring rises from a fine piece of water called Askerne Pool, which was much visited by patients afflicted with rheumatism and other diseases. Bendigo was there under the surveillance of Peter Taylor of Liverpool but Bendigo's attempt to find peace and quiet was not very successful as a large crowd remained encamped outside the place. He had arrived on the Sunday before the fight and many of his friends visited him during his stay and all said how fit he looked - the very picture of health. Bendigo was favourite overnight with odds quoted at 6 to 4.

Caunt at the same time had travelled further afield and was receiving his friends at the Hawke Arms and was attended to by his uncle Ben Butler and Young Molyneaux.

Soon after ten o'clock on the Tuesday morning the representatives of Bell's Life in London made their appearance at the Swan in a post-chaise and drove up to the motley group in front of the house. They recorded the following:

'Our appearance was no doubt suspicious and from the scowling looks of some of the 'hard-ups' with whose private signs we were unacquainted, we were evidently regarded with more fear than affection. At last, recollecting that we had seen Izzy Lazarus down the road and knowing that he is regularly installed as a publican in Sheffield, we asked for him, in order that he might be our cicerone[5] to his friends. Izzy soon made his appearance, being a full stone heavier than when he left town and recognising us, he made known the agreeable intelligence that "'twas t'editor of Bell's Loife in Lunnon" - an announcement so unexpected and apparently so agreeable, that when we descended from our trap we verily believe the sudden appearance of a hippopotamus would not have excited more astonishment. "What", cried one, "is that t'editor of Bell's Loife? Well, I'm dom'd if I didn't take un for a gentleman!" - while another declared he "thought it were summat worse, for he took un for a beak, or summat o' that koind" .

The representatives of Bell's Life visited both men at their respective inns in order to see the state of the two men before the fight. Their report went as follows:

We did not wait to bandy civilities, but proceeded direct to the dormitory of Bendigo, whom we found, like a bacon sandwich, comfortably encased between two slices of flannel, vulgarly called blankets. It was the first time we had the honour of an interview and we made our salaam with due reverence, while the object of our embassy was duly announced by Peter Taylor. Bendigo appeared uncommonly well and was in high spirits. He is a rough, hand-looking fellow, very muscular and we were informed weighed by 11st. 10lb. His seconds, we were informed, were to be Taylor and Nick Ward and, judging from his manner, he seemed to have booked victory as already secure.

Bendigo had taken up his abode in order to be out of the turmoil of the town. He had arrived on the Sunday before and many of his personal friends had been over to see him and on the morning of the fight Bendy held quite a levee. All who knew him and witnessed his first fight with Caunt, pronounced him the very picture of health and condition and he declared that he should give

---

[5] A guide for sightseers.

that 'great chuckle-headed navvy' as he called Ben an easy licking and that he felt that the money was already in his pocket.

To all present we enjoined the expediency of getting early into the ring, as there was a gentle whisper before we left Doncaster that the constables were on the alert. From the Swan we proceeded to the Hawke, where our presence was not less a matter of surprise. We soon obtained an introduction to Caunt, who was assuming his fighting costume. He expressed his joy at seeing us, but proceeded sans cérémonie with the adornment of his person. His father sat by his side and if having a gigantic son is a source of pride he has sufficient to render him doubly so, for the hero of the day proved to be a fine young fellow two-and-twenty years of age, standing six feet three inches in height and weighing fifteen stone and a half, apparently active, strong and full of confidence. There was such an immense difference in stature between the two men and yet Bendigo was the favourite at five and six to four - a state of odds which seemed unaccountable when the disparity in size was considered.

As most of the cavalcade passed through the town of Doncaster on the way to the fight the local inhabitants were soon made aware of the forthcoming event. The whole night long the rattle of wheels, the clattering of horses feet and the shouts of the anxious throng proclaimed the interest which was felt and the wild spirit which was present.

Everyone in the vicinity of Doncaster was impatient to know where the fight was to be held and at eleven o'clock the word spread like wildfire that the Fancy (as the followers of the prize-fights were called) were to take the Selby Road. Off went drags, chaises, gigs, horsemen and pedestrians over the river Don at the foot of the town in pursuit of Jem Crutchley and Bill Fisher who were in charge of the paraphernalia necessary to erect the ring.

Eventually after crossing the river Don and taking a short turn to the right the two men found a suitable spot near the Swan at Askerne where Bendigo had been staying. This route delighted the collector at the adjacent turnpike gate. The ring was formed a short distance from the road, about half way between the Swan and the Hawke. By now the ring was surrounded by a large crowd, many of whom carried sticks of enormous size and did not look an inviting site for anyone who wished to argue with them.

Before the fight could get under way half a dozen horsemen arrived to inform the crowd in an authoritative, but very polite manner that the fight would not

William Thompson - Bendigo

take place. The men on horseback turned out to be a magistrate and a group of constables. The news was not well received by the stick wielding crowd and, faced with this, the magistrate indicated that although he was determined to keep the peace he assured the mob that no further action would be taken against anyone as long as they all left his jurisdiction of the West Riding. As there was nothing else for it but to up stakes and move along in order to avoid arrest, Jem Ward stepped forward to assure the magistrate that his wishes would be respected. Jem took charge of the expedition and after a consultation with other members of the Fancy it was decided to make for Hatfield, a few miles to the south of the spot originally selected.

The two antagonists were now in their respective carriages on the main road, waiting for directions when Jem Ward, stepped forward and informed the protagonists that the next move should be to Hatfield, about seven miles away and within a short run of Lincolnshire. He publicly announced that Hatfield would definitely be the final destination and sent a horseman to the commissary and the men started off to prepare a suitable spot to erect the ring. He was attended by Young Langan, who carried Bendigo's fighting-shoes, Hackett, who was to have been Caunt's second and a numerous cavalcade of charioteers and horsemen, who reached the Bell at Hatfield in quick time. Had his arrangement been adopted all would have gone off well, but unfortunately there were too many masters and too little of a system. A new leader sprang up in the person of Grear, the sporting sweep of Selby, who, being perfectly well acquainted with the localities of the country, as well as anxious to take the fight nearer his own quarters, led the way towards Selby. Followed by a prodigious crowd and by the combatants in their carriages the new commander gave hopes that the ring might be formed before they reached the Ouse, which divided the West from the East Riding. Although several attempts were made it was no go, for the constables kept up with the vanguard and the passage across the Ouse became unavoidable. Those who were able to keep up their steam, however, crossed the bridge over the Ouse into Selby, to the astonishment of the inhabitants and the crowds of market people who were assembled with their wares.

Grear, undismayed, pushed on and knowing every inch of the country did not halt till he got nearly four miles beyond Selby. He then turned down a romantic lane to the left, opposite Skipworth Common and in a large field a few removes from the main road, near the bank of the river, the ring was, with great labour, finally formed. The crowd, which had received fresh accessions from the town of Selby and surrounding country, collected around it.

Many of the original followers failed to reach this distant point and thousands were thus deprived of the object of their long and wearisome journey. Many complained that had Ward's directions been obeyed it would have brought them nearer home, with a more certain chance of proceeding to business without interruption.

While original followers were dropped during the long journey, new followers were also collected along the way, including several members of the Badsworth Hunt. They came up in scarlet, headed by Captain B., one of the right sort, who backed Bendigo at six to four, before he proceeded to borrow the mackintosh cape from the man with whom he placed the bet.

Having taken breath, all prepared for action and the ring was beaten out with as much effect as so sudden and unceremonious an assemblage would permit. The men entered the ring about half-past five o'clock with Bendigo taking the lead, attended by Peter Taylor and Nick Ward. He was in high spirits, but on calling for his spiked shoes, was informed that they had unfortunately been sent on to Hatfield and thus he had the disadvantage of adopting less suitable 'crab-shells[6]', a circumstance which did not seem, however, to disturb his equanimity. Caunt then came forward waited upon by Young Molyneaux and Gregson. On peeling, their condition seemed admirable and the flush of expected victory animated their 'dials'. Two umpires and a referee having been chosen, all was ready and the fight commenced.

THE FIGHT

Round 1:
Bendigo immediately began to dodge backward and forward in order to draw Ben in and then hit him with his right as soon as he advanced, but Ben was having none of it. When Bendigo feinted to hit a blow with his right and then hit Ben with a good shot on the left eye, Caunt immediately moved in and threw his arms around Bendigo and began to squeeze the breath out of him. As Caunt tried to throw him, Bendigo wriggled free and realising he would always come second in a trial of strength fell to the ground and safety, ending the round.

---

[6] Shoes

Round 2:
At the start of the second round Caunt's face was flushed due to the blow to the eye in the first and the look on his face as he came out made it clear he was keen to return to the battle. Ben immediately swung left and right catching Bendigo with both blows but Bendigo escaped with Caunt chasing him. It was then Bendigo's turn, as Big Ben moved ponderously forward throwing a tremendous blow at his opponent's head. He ducked to avoid it and then, getting under Ben's guard gave him a terrific belt in the mouth that at once set the blood flowing. Caunt decided not to stand and be 'picked off' by these shots and moved in, grabbed hold of Bendigo and after a bit of a struggle picked Bendigo up and threw him.

Round 3:
Out they came again with Bendigo ducking and dodging in order to avoid the huge powerful arm of Ben, until he eventually saw a chance and planted a good shot with his left onto Ben's mouth. This riled Ben who rushed at his man and got another hold on him, swung him around and then threw him to the ground before falling on top of him. This was not popular with the crowd, but it was fair and in accordance with the rules of the Prize Ring.

Round 4:
When they emerged for the fourth round Bendigo still appeared dazed from the previous round and so used all his dodging skills to buy himself time to recover. For a full five minutes not a blow was struck by either man and the spectators became very agitated and shouted out to the men to "Get to work; don't keep us here all night". Both men exchanged blows but with none hitting their target. Eventually, Bendigo throwing shots as he wisely moved away caught Caunt a tremendous crack on the cheek, which once again drew the claret. Once again Caunt's response was to rush impulsively after his opponent and quite a rally followed in which lefts and rights were exchanged. Caunt finally managed to close in on Bendigo, where he always had the huge advantage of his strength which he demonstrated again by picking his man up, before throwing him and falling on top of him.
When both men were picked up by their seconds it could be seen that they both had badly damaged noses. Caunt's bled profusely along with a cut under his left eye, while Bendigo's nose was swollen from a visitation from Caunt's right fist. The seconds worked well on their men though and both were ready to continue when "Time" was called.

Round 5:
The fifth round began with the two men sparring until Caunt, tired of Bendigo's style of 'hit and run', moved in close, seized his man in a vice like grip against the ropes, almost strangling him. Eventually Bendigo began to work his way free so Caunt threw him and fell on him.

Rounds 6-11:
These rounds continued the trend of the previous five with the difference in stature of the two men dictating their tactics, with Bendigo the smaller but faster of the two men, forever hitting and moving and marking Caunt's face quite extensively and, although not liked by the crowd, he would drop to the floor to end the round whenever Ben got hold of him when the fighting brought the two men close together. Caunt on the other hand, was much the bigger and stronger, but also the more ponderous and so his 'game plan' was to get in close as soon as possible (knowing he would be taking blows as he came in) and use his greater strength to hit, squeeze and throw his opponent. Both styles have their merits with Bendigo being acclaimed as the better technical boxer, while it was generally accepted that had he not gone down to earth regularly to avoid Ben he would surely have lost the fight before the twelfth round.

Round 12:
Battle commenced with both men raring to go. As Bendigo had been missing Caunt's head a lot recently he decided to aim more for his body and commenced left and rights to his trunk with the hits sounding like a big drum. After taking a left under his right eye Caunt instantly closed in and a violent struggle ensued which ended with both men falling to the floor.

Round 13:
Caunt was determined not to allow Bendigo's 'hit and run' tactics and immediately rushed to his man, hit him right and left before grappling with him at close quarters. Once he had Bendigo in his arms, to stop him falling he carried him to the ropes against which he squeezed him with such force as to almost kill him. So terrible was the force brought to bear upon his antagonist, that Bendigo was almost deprived of sense and motion. Caunt's fingers were round his throat and the whole of his massive frame was pressing Bendy against the stake. The spectators, disgusted at this mode of fighting, which was certainly more unmanly and objectionable than Bendy's dropping tactics, grew furious and yelled out to Caunt; "Thou big, ugly toad: dost thou call that foightin'? Whoy, the little 'un would lick thee and two or three more such if

thee'd nobbut foight fair." Ben's savage blood was up, however and be cared not a jot for their remonstrances. He had got the man who had been hitting him such stinging blows for the last six rounds in his power and he didn't mean to let him go till he had squelched the life out of him. That, at least, seemed to be his object, for he was mad with cruel fury and was gloating fiendishly over poor Bendy's livid features, which were absolutely purple from the awful pressure on his windpipe. In vain the people shouted "Let him go; he'll be killed!" Bendigo's neck was over the ropes and no doubt there would have been an end to Mr. William Thompson's career had not a rush been made by some of his friends, who with their clasped knives cut the ropes. One account says that be was nearly dead and that when carried to his corner the blood was oozing from his ears. The mob made a rush for the ring and it was evident that they meant mischief and that Caunt would have been very roughly handled had not the ringkeepers surrounded him and beaten them off. Bendigo's followers, the Nottingham Lambs, were mustered in great force and were furious at the manner in which their Bold Bendigo had been handled. As it was, the confusion can be better imagined than described. Referee and umpires were swept away from the ring and a free fight ensued in which fists, sticks and whips were freely used. Fortunately the ringkeepers were numerous and worked together and ultimately beat the crowd back. when an attempt was made to repair the ring. This was found to be impossible, so the men had to continue the battle with one side open. Of course, the time occupied in the melee was an advantage to Bendigo, who, having been attended to by his seconds, had somewhat recovered, although still very shaky when the men toed the scratch once more.

Round 14-49:
During these rounds the greatest confusion prevailed while Bendigo persevered with his getting down tactics as he had had enough of Caunt's embraces and set about studiously avoiding them.

During this stage of the fight a magistrate made an appearance with the idea of ending the hostilities, but he had no chance and was forced to retire, no doubt feeling that amidst such a scene, the dignity of his office would not be properly vindicated.

Round 50ish:
In approximately the fiftieth round Caunt claimed the fight saying that Bendigo had kicked him while he lay on the ground and an appeal was made to the referee, he declared he saw nothing unfair and the fight continued.

So great was the disturbance around the ring that it was a wonder the men were able to fight at all and every moment it was expected that ropes, stakes, seconds and principals would all be swept away.

Round 75ish:
Bendigo's hitting was still terrific, but still Caunt was game to the backbone and, although heavily punished, fought with him and when he caught him gave him the advantage of his 'Cornish hug'. Both men were alternately distressed but the powerful hitting of Bendigo made him still the favourite even though he had received some heavy body hits and was somewhat exhausted by Caunt's hugging and hanging on to him.

Last round
In the last round on "Time" being called, both men came ready to the scratch, when Caunt prepared for his rush, Bendigo went to the floor 'without a blow'. Bendigo's friends described this as a slip while Molyneaux, Caunt's second cried "Foul" and claimed the battle. An appeal was made to the referee who decided that Bendigo had gone down without a blow and declared Caunt the winner, at which point Molyneaux threw his hat into the air and claimed the battle. The fight had lasted one hour and twenty minutes.

An unbelievable row followed, with the friends of Bendigo declaring he had gone down from accident owing to his substitute shoes being without spikes. Bendigo was indignant and was ready to carry on, but it was all over, the referee had given the fight to Caunt so Molyneaux escorted his man from the ring. Bendigo, in desperation, seized the colours and in turn tried to claim the win and chaos continued. Caunt was conveyed to his carriage only to be dragged out by the Nottingham Lambs, in order to renew the fight but his friends declined and placed him on a horse, only for him to be pulled off again and but for the protection of his own followers he would have been very badly beaten. In the end he had to walk to Selby from where he was taken back to the Hawke Arms, where his wounds were dressed and every attention paid him and although dreadfully punished he remained strong and vigorous.

After the battle Bendigo proceeded to Selby where he stayed the night. He appeared little the worse for wear so far as hitting was concerned. The only marks were a flush under the right eye, a swelling under the left ear, some marks on the lower part of the right shoulder blade and other excoriations and abrasions of the cuticle, bearing full evidence of the sever squeezing and scrapings on the ropes inflicted by the bruin-like hugs of his huge antagonist.

On 15th of April Bell's Life in London stated that it had received several letters from the friends of the two fighters arguing their respective cases and members of the Fancy who had placed bets on various categories of the fight needed the results officially declaring as bets had not yet been paid out. The results were announced as follows: Caunt was awarded the 'first knock down', while Bendigo was said to have drawn 'first blood' and Caunt given the fight verdict as Bendigo went down without a blow, which was confirmed later by the referee and all bets were paid out on these decisions. The matter was to be decided once and for all when the two umpires and the referee were due to meet at the house of a Mr Hutchinson the next day, the 16th.

With regard to Bendigo's misfortune in being deprived of his spiked shoes, while this is admitted, it is stated on the part of Caunt that he was also deprived of his second, (Hackett), his water, brandy and other things which, like Bendigo's shoes were carried to Hatfield. The progress to Selby is attributed to the magistrates, who, it is said, recommended all parties to go out of the West Riding - careless where the fight took place so long as it did not occur within their bailiwick.

A week later, on 22nd of April, Bell's Life in London published the following letters covering the meeting of the referee and umpires on the 16th of April at Mr Hutchinson's house.

We have received the following final decision respecting this match. There can now be no difficulty in the stakeholder giving up the battle-money, according to the award of the referee and one umpire. Allowing that the other umpire had been consulted and gave it as his opinions that the conduct of Bendigo had been perfectly fair it was still two against one against him. The rules of the Prize Ring in these matters are imperative. The articles specified that the two umpires and a referee should be chosen on the ground and in the event of dispute the judgement of the latter to be final. Two umpires and a referee were chosen and although the umpires did not compare opinions, the appeal was made to the referee, who acting on the belief that there was a dispute, decided according to the best of his judgement, as he was justified in doing, more especially under the circumstances in which he was placed. Further wrangling would be absurd and the only way is after the battle-money has been given up to make a fresh match and secure better order in future.

TO THE EDITOR OF BELL'S LIFE IN LONDON.

Sir - I transmit you the following decision of one of the umpires and of the referee, respecting the late fight between Caunt and Bendigo; the other umpire appeared at my house on Monday and was asked repeatedly, in my presence, by the friends of Caunt, his decision respecting the fight, as also his name, but, by the advice of Bendigo's friends, he declined giving either, with the exception of his having admitted that Bendigo went down without a blow being given or received by either party, but would not say whether accidental or to avoid punishment - I now give you a copy of the communications I received, viz.:-

Frithwood,
April 16, 1838.

Sir - I could not positively get to Dronfield today, but you know my decision about the fight. Caunt is the winner through Bendigo's dropping without a blow being struck by either of them.

I am, &c.
JAMES CLARKE, Umpire
Spring Grove,
April 12, 1838.

Mr Hutchinson - Since I wrote to you I have seen one of Mr Caunt's friends, also Bendigo and several of his friends; yesterday they both informed me that they had agreed to meet at your house on Monday next on which day I could not possibly go, as it is a busy day, preparing goods for the market on the following day.

With respect to the decision which I gave respecting the late fight, I can say neither more nor less than I said before - that it was and is my candid opinion that Bendigo went down to avoid punishment, without a blow being given or received by either of them. I can assure you that I say it without any partiality whatever. Bendigo's friends desired I would mention in my letter that, previous to the fight, I had made a small bet, upon honour, of five shillings that Bendigo would win the fight. When the parties made choice of me Molyneaux asked me if I had made any bets, which I said I had not; I at the moment forgot the small bet I had made previous to the fight; but had it been £5, or five times £5 would not have biased me to have acted partially to either of the parties. To put the matter in as tangible a shape and in as little compass as possible my decision is that Bendigo's going down to avoid punishment was foul and Caunt is entitled to the stakes. I conclude by saying, that neither

flattery nor threats will cause me to change my opinion or decision upon the subject; therefore, this will be the last communication you may expect from me; and this is the first and last time that I will ever take any part in a prize-fight. Give my respects to Mr. Clarke, the umpire, if he is present on Monday next. - I trust this will meet the approbation of the umpires, especially Mr Clarke; the other person I don't know, besides I had no conversation with him when the fight terminated, nor did I see him at all.
I am, &c. WM LOCKWOOD, Referee

I can assure you that the parties whose communication I have transmitted to you are highly respectable gentlemen and in my opinion would not tell an untruth, the other umpire I know nothing of - I therefore sincerely hope that the parties will feel satisfied with your decision in 'Bell's Life' of Sunday next.
I am, &c. W HUTCHINSON
Swan Inn
Dronfield

After this the stake-holder handed over the battle-money to Caunt, with the following observations:- The referee's decision must be upheld and if in his judgement Bendigo went down (he says, in fact, fell to avoid), then it is admitted that although he had the best of the battle - Caunt is entitled to the stakes and pro tem to the title of 'Champion'.

The question of who was rightfully champion was often open to debate. Despite the stakeholders comments here Caunt was not generally regarded as champion at this time.

The next week Bendigo entered into articles with Caunt for £100 a side, to come off on the 30th of July but when £40 a side had been deposited, a forfeit took place, under the following circumstances:-

The Deaf 'Un, as James Burke was usually called, had returned from America, in the height of his popularity and his challenges to 'any man in or out of England', especially 'Mister Bendy', proved too strong a 'red herring' across the trail for the Nottingham man to resist. He forfeited the £40 cash down to grasp at what proved, for a time, a fleeting shadow, as the Deaf 'Un, after his challenge and its acceptance went on a Parisian tour. It was not until Shrove Tuesday (February 12th 1839) that Bendigo and Burke had their 'cock-shy' at Appleby and Bendigo thereafter received a much disputed champions belt from Jem Ward at Liverpool.

Chapter 4

THE BATTLE WITH BRASSEY

(1839-1840)

The remainder of 1838 and the whole of 1839, passed without Caunt sporting his colours in the lists. Although Caunt did not take part in fighting, the newspapers were rife with challenges from Caunt to Bendigo and Bendigo to Caunt. Each 'champion' roving about the counties in which he was most popular having benefits arranged for them by their supporters. Each arrived with a 'star' company and each awakening the city or town where his company performed with a thundering challenge, while each pugilistic planet revolved in his own particular orbit without giving the other a chance of a collision.

In this interval Jem Ward presented a champion's belt to Bendigo, at the Queen's Theatre, Liverpool, amid great acclamations and again the tiresome game of challenging and making appointments for a meeting to draw up articles at places where the challenged party never attended or meant to show, went on. Brassey, of Bradford, too, having in the interim beaten Young Langan, of Liverpool and Jem Bailey, put in his claim and joined the chorus of challengers. Burke also offered himself for £100, which Bendigo declined.

In the latter half of 1839 the following appeared in Bell's Life:

To the Editor of BELL'S LIFE IN LONDON.

SIR, Caunt states that he has been given to understand I wish to have another trial with him for £200 a side and that his money is ready at any sporting house in Sheffield. Now, Sir, I have been to many houses that he frequents and cannot find any one to put any money down in his behalf and as he was in Sheffield for a fortnight previous to going away to second Renwick. I think, if he meant fighting, he would have made the match when we were both in Sheffield. Now, Sir, what I mean to say is this; I will fight Caunt or any other man in England, for from £200 to £500 a side and I hope I shall not be disappointed as I mean fighting and nothing else; and to convince the patrons of the Prize Ring that there is no empty chaff about me, as I am going to leave Sheffield this week my money will be ready any day or hour at Mr. Edward

John Leechman – better known as "Brassey"

Daniels', 'Three Crowns,' Parliament Street, Nottingham. Or if Burke wants another shy, I will fight him for £150 a side.

WILLIAM THOMPSON, alias BENDIGO.

This certainly looked like business, yet the next week Caunt declares; 'I will make a match with Bendigo for £200 and I will take a sovereign to go to Nottingham, or give Bendigo the same if he will meet me at Lazarus's house at Sheffield.' This was in July and shortly after Bendigo writes:

To the Editor of BELL'S LIFE IN LONDON

MR EDITOR: Having sent a letter to Caunt accepting his challenge on his own terms and not receiving an answer, I wish to put that bounceable gentleman's intentions to a public test. I am willing to fight him on his own terms and I will give him the sovereign he requires to pay his expenses in coming to Nottingham to make the match and let it be as early as possible. As to Deaf Burke, he is but of minor importance to me. I have no objection to give him another chance to regain his lost laurel and will fight him for his 'cool hundred,' as he calls it, providing he or his friends make the first deposit of £50, for my friends are not willing to stake less. Should the above not suit either of these aspirants for fistic fame, I again repeat I will fight any man in the world for £200 or £500, barring neither weight, country, nor colour.
I am always to be heard of at the Three Crowns, Parliament Street, Nottingham.
WILLIAM THOMPSON alias BENDIGO: -
August 3, 1839

Brassey, meanwhile, was temporarily removed from these discussions by an accident beyond his own control. The magistrates of Salford, determining to suppress pugilism so far as they could, indicted Brassey for riot in seconding Sam Pixton in a fight with Jones, of Manchester and obtaining a conviction, sentenced him to two months' incarceration in the borough gaol. He was thus placed 'hors de combat[7]'.

Early in 1840 Bendigo was in London, with his headquarters at Jem Burn's, where Nick Ward exhibited with him the gloves in friendly emulation.

---

[7] Out of action

Nick Ward, the brother of the ex-champion Jem, was however, averse to any closer engagement. Bendigo returned to the provinces and the next week the public was informed that 'Caunt's money, to be made into a stake of £200, was lying at Tom Spring's, but nothing has been heard from Bendigo'

All these arrangements came to nothing though with the news that on 23rd of March 1840 Bendigo had suffered an accident that would keep him out of boxing action for quite some time – if indeed he was ever fit enough to return at all.

Bendigo, who was always a careless, devil-may-care sort of a fellow, fond of practical joking and clowning of all kinds, or any caper which would provoke a laugh from his comrades, was returning from the military steeplechases held near Nottingham. When they arrived close to the Pender's House, on the London Road on his return home he and his companions were cracking their jokes about having a steeplechase among themselves. Bendy exclaimed, "Now, boys, I'll show you how to run a steeplechase without falling", he at once threw a somersault and on alighting, fell down and he attempted in vain three times to rise from the ground. His companions, thinking for the moment he was joking laughed heartily, but discovering it was no joke went to his assistance and raised him up but the poor fellow had no use of his left leg. A gig was sent for immediately, in which he was conveyed to the house of his brother and Messrs. Wright and Thompson. Surgeons were immediately called in and on examination of the knee they pronounced the injury to the cap to be of so serious a nature that there is likelihood he could be lame for life.

Tragic as the accident was, it left the way open for the likes of Caunt, Nick Ward and Brassey to eye the championship for themselves.

Ned Painter writes thus, at the end of July:-

MR. EDITOR, - In answer to an observation made in last week's paper, that 'providing Brassey's friends will sustain their promises', allow me to say that 'corn', not 'chaff', is the answer of Brassey to Caunt. Brassey went to Liverpool to make the match with Hampson; when he arrived there neither man nor money was to be seen. When Caunt challenged the whole world, Brassey and his friends accepted the challenge and to meet Caunt's wish, sent £25 to Tom Spring a week previous to the day appointed. I went myself on the very day, but Caunt and his party were invisible. If Caunt means a fight and not a farce, he must go to Leeds or come to Norwich and match at his own

expense this time, as neither Brassey nor myself were allowed even the £2 for expenses promised. I am Mr. Editor, for work, not mere words or wind.
Norwich, July 30th, 1840.
NED PAINTER

To which Peter Crawley thus replied on behalf of Caunt: -

SIR, - My having placed £25 in your hands will, I hope, remove all doubt as regards Caunt's money being ready; and it remains with the friends of Brassey alone to appoint a day, either Monday, Tuesday or Wednesday week, through the medium of your paper, to meet at my house, to draw up articles and put down their dust; and unless this be attended to, for my part I shall consider they do not mean business. I have taken the responsibility on myself of detaining the money, a little longer; that would give Brassey time to pin his friends at Norwich, which, I understand, is all that prevents the match being made now.

I am, &c., P. CRAWLEY
Queen's Head and French Horn,
Duke Street, West Smithfield.
August 21st, 1840.

So, in August 1840, with Ned Painter acting on behalf of Brassey in Norwich, and Peter Crawley in London looking after Ben's interests, the two men attempted to fix up a match between the fighters. All difficulties were eventually sorted out and a match for £100 a side was made. The fight was to take place on 26th of October 1840. As the deposits were made good and the day of the fight approached, the interest in sporting circles rose to an intense height and at the payment of the last deposit at Tom Spring's Castle Tavern it was literally stormed by eager crowds.

It was on the evening of September 28th, 1840, that an unusual foregathering took place at the Castle Tavern, Holborn. There was evidently something unusual 'on the tapis[8]', because the old parlour, beloved by sportsmen, was crowded with the cream of the London Fancy, both professional and amateur. There were veteran ring-goers present, who had seen Mendoza fight Jackson for the Championship in 1795 and had been present at all the great battles since that event. There were also young bloods having their first introduction

---

[8] A rumour that something is about to happen.

to London life. There were well-known bookmakers, fashionable jockeys and pugilistic celebrities of all weights and ages. This representative company had assembled to give a hearty welcome to their old friend, Ned Painter, the only man who had ever beaten Tom Spring. Ned had come up from Norwich and had brought with him his young protege Brassey, of Bradford, who had accepted the challenge thrown down by big Ben Caunt.

The occasion of the meeting was the third and final deposit in the match that had been made for £200. It was a jolly evening, according to one account and the greeting Ned Painter received was tremendous as he entered and took his seat on the right of his old antagonist, Tom Spring, who was in the chair, whilst Brassey sat on the worthy host's left. Mr. Vincent Dowling, editor of Bell's Life, proposed the health of Ned Painter (or Flat Nose as he was called in Norwich), which was given three times and with musical honours. Then Painter got on his pedestals and asked the company to drink to his dear old friend, Tom Spring, after thanking them for the warm welcome he had received. The cheering which followed Ned's speech and continued until Tom got on his feet to return thanks must have startled passers-by in Holborn. With beaming face he told how delighted he was to see an old opponent under his roof, the only man that had ever plucked the laurel from his brow, a reflection however, that in no respect diminished the pleasure of the interview. He said he thought the true character of the British pugilist was founded on the fact that the moment a battle was decided all animosity ceased between the combatants and their friendship was riveted the tighter. This manly sentiment was received with loud cheers, emphasised as it was by the two old antagonists standing up and shaking hands cordially with one another.

Then the business of the evening was attended to; Ned Painter putting down the money for Brassey and Peter Crawley doing ditto for Caunt. An announcement was made by Tom Spring, that Brassey would take his benefit on the following Monday at the Bloomsbury Assembly Rooms and give the Fancy a taste of his quality with the gloves. After that the remainder of the evening was given up to harmony with the meeting continuing until the early hours of the following morning.

At the benefit on the following Monday, too, there was a tremendous muster and certainly Brassey must have been more than satisfied with the enthusiastic reception accorded him. Earls, right honourables and baronets assembled to see what the big Yorkshireman could do and his set-to with the gloves - Tom Spring being his antagonist - was watched with no end of interest. Of course,

Brassey's style was coarse and rough, as compared with that of the scientific, graceful master of the art. Yet he impressed the company with the idea that he could hit hard and that he was quick enough to give a lot of trouble to any man who stood up to him.

The following poem was printed in the sporting journals of the day and would have livened up the columns of matter of fact reports and challenges.

AN HEROIC EPISTLE FROM BRASSEY TO BEN CAUNT

> To thee I send these lines, illustrious Caunt!
> Of courage tried and huge as John of Gaunt,
> To thee my foolscap with black ink I blot,
> To tell the Big 'Un Brassey fears him not,
>
> And that in battle, should the fates allow,
> He means to snatch the laurels from his brow,
> At all his boasted pluck and prowess smile,
> And give him pepper in superior style.
>
> Yes, gallant Caunt, next Tuesday will declare
> If you or I the Champion's belt shall wear;
> And be assured, regardless of the tin,
> I'll go to work and do my best to win,
>
> Prove that in fight one Briton can surpass ye,
> And if you ask his name, I thunder - Brassey!
> What proof of milling prowess did you show
> In your two scrambling fights with Bendigo?
>
> When of your foeman's punishment aware,
> You roughly squeezed him like a polar bear,
> Nearly extinguished in his lungs the breath,
> And almost hugged him in your arms to death
>
> Such a base system I pronounce humbugging;
> Don't call it fighting, Caunt, I call it hugging,
> And if bold Brassey with that game you tease,
> The bear may soon be minus of his grease,

And for a practice cowardly as foul,
Receive a lesson that may make him growl.
But bounce I bar - plain dealing is my plan,
And in the ring I'll meet you man to man,
And do, most certainly, the best I can.

May no base beak, or trap with aspect rude,
Upon a comfortable mill intrude -
A mill between not enemies, but friends,
And upon which a lot of blunt depends;

A mill, I trust, which, as in days of yore,
Will honest fighting to the ring restore;
A mill which, whosoe'er may win the same,
Will show the British boxer's genuine game,

Unkind aspersions on the Fancy crush,
And put accurs'd knife-practice to the blush -
A practice which, with bold and fearless face,
In bloody letters stamps our land's disgrace !

But let that pass, while we, like boxers bold,
Shall manly contest in the ring uphold,
And settle matters, not with slaughtering knives,
But well-braced muscles and a bunch of fives.

What tho' in battle with some Fancy lad
An ogle should in mourning suit be clad?
What tho' profusion of straightforward knocks
Should for a while confuse the knowledge box?

Why, these are trifles which a cur may scare,
But teach good men hard punishment to bear;
And as they pass this early region thro'
All men will have a clumsy thump or two,

And there's no doubt 'twill lessen their complaining
To meet hard knocks to get them into training;
But Time, my worthy, warns me to desist,
So for a while farewell, my man of fist;

> Of your conceit on Tuesday I will strip ye -
> On Tuesday next "I meet you at Philippi;"
> Till then believe me resolute and saucy,
> A foe without one hostile feeling -
> "BRASSEY"

Brassey was an aspirant for the Championship whose real name was John Leechman and he was born in Bradford on January 1st 1815. His average weight during his Ring career was around 12st and his first battle recorded was with Thomas Hartley, for £2 a side, at Eccles Moor in 1831, with Brassey winning in one hour and fifteen minutes. He next met and defeated Ned Batterson for the extraordinary sum of £3 5s a side, the men fighting seventy-two rounds in one hour and fifty-two minutes. He afterwards fought and beat George Ireson, of Salford near Manchester, for £6 a side, in the May of 1883. In the same month he fought Young Winterflood, of Nottingham, a well-known clever pugilist, but after doing battle for upwards of an hour they ended with a wrangle, and a draw was the result. On April 24th, 1836, he defeated Jem Bailey for £10 a side and in the January of the following year beat Tom Scrutton for £20 a side, in seventeen rounds. Then came his defeat by Bendigo, which took place near Sheffield on May 24th, 1836 and was for £26 a side. He fought Jem Bailey for £25 a side, at Hales Green, near Pulham, Norfolk and beat him; Bailey, however, sued the stakeholder and recovered the money. Then came his battle for £60 a side, with Young Langan, whom he defeated in seventy-five rounds at Woodhead, Cheshire on October 8th, 1839. This was Brassey's last encounter prior to the match with Ben Caunt, which is about to be described.

Certainly, he had not fought many first-rate men, yet his encounter with Young Langan was looked upon as a great performance and brought his name prominently before the public. Accompanied by his guide, mentor and friend, Mat Robinson, he visited Liverpool, Manchester, Leeds, Sheffield, Bradford, Hull and Nottingham, taking benefits everywhere and pulling in large sums of money and he declared that he intended to throw down the gauntlet for the Championship as soon as he could raise the necessary £200.

With the details agreed, the match was made with Ben Caunt and the deposits paid down punctually to Tom Spring, at the Castle, who acted as stakeholder and Six Mile Bottom, Cambridgeshire, (distinguished in former times by the contests of the dons of the local university) was chosen to be the site of the fight.

The place chosen for the battle was also a classic one in the annals of the Prize Ring for it was the valley of Six Mile Bottom, between Cambridge and Newmarket, where John Gully had thrashed Bob Gregson in the autumn of 1807. Although probably inferior in natural boxing skills to bygone heroes, the present competitors were not less great in their own estimation and certainly quite as great in bulk - for Caunt stood 6ft.2in and weighed 14st.7lb and Brassey, two inches shorter, weighed 12st.1lb. (a standard which, according to the best judges of the time, was sufficient for all useful purposes in the Prize Ring, all beyond that being deemed surplus to requirements). In point of age they were pretty much upon a par and in the prime of life, Caunt having been born in March 1814 and Brassey in the month of January in the following year.

The opinion of Bendigo as to the merits of the two men was naturally sought and he, without hesitation, gave the 'palm' to Brassey, whom he pronounced the better tactician, although not necessarily the gamer man. As provincial champions they were held in high estimation - Brassey at Leeds, Bradford and those districts and Caunt at Nottingham, Sheffield and the surrounding country.

However, their pretensions as scientific men were viewed with little favour - and in fact, in that respect their acquirements were but of an inferior character - as their sparring displays with the accomplished Tom Spring sufficiently demonstrated. Still, although rough, they were deemed ready and a slashing fight was anticipated.

Brassey 'took his breathings' with Ned Painter, at Norwich, whilst Caunt trained in company with Peter Crawley, near Hatfield. The mere fact that these two men, Painter and Crawley, were retained to look after the warriors was sufficient guarantee that all was fair and above board and proof that the contest would be fought out on its merits and it was impossible for men to have been brought to the 'post' in better condition, or with a stronger feeling of personal confidence. But the interest taken in this contest for the Championship was much keener than usual. Old stagers raked up their recollections of Gully and Gregson, of Cribb and Molineaux, of Harry Pearce and Jem Belcher, of Spring and Langan and Jem Ward and Simon Byrne and, after the fashion of old stagers, of course, were unanimous in declaring that these two new big 'uns were far inferior to the giants of a previous generation. But still Brassey and Caunt were giants and nobody could deny that they were

Peter Crawley – Caunt's trainer

exceptionally big and powerful men and in those days, as today, size when fighting counted for a great deal.

As on all these occasions the betting was influenced by local prejudices; and while at Leeds, Bradford and their vicinities, the 'Yorkshire tyke' (Brassey) was the favourite at five to four, in Sheffield, Nottingham, Newmarket and London, Caunt had the call at six and seven to four and finally at two to one and five to two, at which price large sums were laid out.

The date selected was that of the Newmarket Houghton Meeting and the time fixed was between eight and nine o'clock in the morning of the 26th, so that it should not interfere with those who desired to kill two birds with one stone and be in time for the racing. So on the Monday both men left their training quarters, Brassey journeying with Ned Painter to Newmarket and putting up at the Queen Victoria, whilst Caunt went to Littlebury, in Essex, only a few miles from the Metropolis of the Turf.

Long before the specified time for the fight Tom Oliver, assisted by Clarke and others, had the roped arena fixed up. On this occasion the ropes were new and the stakes of extra thickness, in consideration of the Herculean proportions of the brace of heavyweights who were to perform within the magic circle. The coming throng formed a circle of ample dimensions around the all-important arena, quickly surrounding the ring. Every moment the crowd increased in density and included in its motley features a vast concourse of the Turf aristocracy and not a few of the right sort, who had posted from London to participate in the amusements of the day. The remainder, to the extent of 2,000 or 3,000 was of that mingled character which it would be difficult to particularise, many of them being so disguised in their storm-defying protectors as to give them the advantage of perfect incognito, combined with personal protection.

There was a very large muster of spectators, amongst them a number of foreigners, who had come down to the races, but who had never before witnessed a real genuine British prize-fight. Amongst those present, were a distinguished audience of sportsmen and a number of undergraduates from Cambridge University who came in style in drags and fours.

The following is a list of a few present:- The Duke of Beaufort, with his son, the Marquis of Worcester, the Marquis of Exeter, the Earls of Chesterfield and Jersey, Lord George Bentinck and Lord Henry Fitzroy, Sir John Shelley, the

Hon. General Grosvenor, the Bon Captain Rous (better known as the Admiral), Charles Greville, George Payne, 'Fullar' Craven, Delmé Radcliffe, Tom Crommelin, Colonel Peel, Will Ridsdale and Mr. John Gully. It was the day of the big Cambridgeshire race, which in itself attracted all these thorough sportsmen, who could not resist a good mill in whatever weather. Then there was a great muster of fighting men present - Jem Burn, Johnny Hannan, Johnny Broome, Dan Dismore, Johnny Walker, Young Dutch Sam and a host of others, all with their circles of admirers. There was Bendigo there, too, limping about on crutches, but still as light-hearted and comical as ever.

Unusually for a prize-fight, on this occasion the usual secrecy of the fight details had not been observed, for it was thought that, with the racing being on, very little notice would be taken of a large assemblage of sportsmen. Unfortunately, however, the news that the fight was to take place on the Tuesday reached the ears of a gentleman who had a fanatical aversion to the Prize Ring and all its followers. This was the Rector of Cheveley, who was also a Justice of the Peace. He declared that the fight should not take place if he could help it. But in the parlour of the Queen Victoria a secret conclave was held, at which Jem Burn, Peter Crawley, Ned Painter, Tom Spring, Young Molyneaux, Johnny Broome, Dick Curtis and Old Tom Oliver were present and at which a scheme was devised to throw the reverend gentleman off the scent.

Monday had been fine but cold, but on the Tuesday morning the rain came down in torrents. This however, does not appear to have dampened the ardour of the sportsmen, who had flocked to Newmarket, attracted by the racing, the fight, or both and rarely had the capital of horse racing been so full. Perhaps the presence of the Queen and Prince Albert had caused many to arrive, although, of courage, none of that class knew or cared much about the battle. They were there to support a fancy bazaar, which had been opened in aid of the medical charities of the place. According to report, in spite of the inclement weather, the streets were full of vehicles and pedestrians soon after daybreak and the greatest bustle and excitement prevailed.

The only dread was that the police and the magistrate would appear upon the scene. But the little ruse decided upon on the previous evening worked exceedingly well. A messenger was sent to the Rector of Cheveley, who declared that he had come from the Chief Constable of Newmarket and that he was instructed to inform the reverend gentleman that the fight was to take place at Mildenhall, in Suffolk. His reverence, it would appear, fell into the trap readily enough because he arose immediately, although it was only about six in the morning and having sworn in a posse of special constables, proceeded at once in the direction of Mildenhall. Once there he patiently awaited the arrival of the 'breakers of the peace,' whom he was resolved to prosecute with the utmost rigour of the law. For hours did that unfortunate parson and his posse keep vigilant watch in the pelting rain, scouring the lanes in every direction and maintaining a perfect cordon of outposts all round the village of Mildenhall. Yet no sight of the approaching enemy rewarded their patient vigil and the credulous 'beak' did not return to Newmarket until the fight was over, a victim to the clever hoax that had been perpetrated.

Upon the appearance of the parson of Cheveley at the magisterial divan in Newmarket on the same day, after the fight, to deplore the hoax of which he had been made the victim, his vicissitudes produced a good deal of fun and not a little commendation of the ingenious concocter of the hoax to which he had fallen so simple a victim.

In order that the Fancy could enjoy a day's racing after the fight it was stipulated in the articles that the fighters should be in the ring between eight and nine o'clock that morning. Brassey was first to arrive at the ring and after a substantial wait Caunt was still nowhere to be seen and the spectators were becoming very impatient for his arrival as they were sitting and standing in the torrential rain. The time limit of nine o'clock was approaching and people were beginning to talk of Caunt's non arrival and the possibility of Brassey claiming a 'walk over' by 'walking over the course' and claiming forfeit, which would obviously have been a tremendous disappointment to the thousands in the crowd after all their efforts to attend the big fight.

At five minutes to nine Caunt arrived and a buzz of anticipation swept through the huge crowd. Without any waste of time the two gladiators were manoeuvred into the ring, Caunt attended by Peter Crawley, Dick Curtis and Young Molyneaux and Brassey esquired by Ned Painter, Jem Hall and Johnny Broome, which created a lot of amusement to see two such big men seconded by such comparatively small ones.

An inner circle of the privileged was soon formed by those who chose to 'qualify' by taking out certificates at five shillings each from the Commissary. For the accommodation of these a quantity of straw had been spread a few yards from the ring, but such was its saturated state, from the continued rain, that it afforded little protection and carriage seats and gig cushions were in general request. Never was the recent invention of waterproof clothing more prized.

On entering the ring Caunt was wearing a large Welsh wig which, when removed, disclosed his closely cropped hair and with his tremendous ears and high cheekbones he looked by no means a prepossessing person. Caunt approached Brassey and offered to lay him a private bet on the outcome of the fight, but the Yorkshireman, who at the best of times was none too good tempered took it as just an offensive piece of bounce and turned away from him with a scowl.

Mr Vincent Dowling accepted the post of referee and the two umpires were also chosen, the 'colours' of the 'yellowmen', (as both fighters had chosen the same colour) were tied to the stake and all prepared for action.

On stripping, the gigantic frame of Caunt struck the uninitiated with surprise. His superior height and weight left no room for nice calculations and his broad back and muscular developments had a most formidable look while his long arms and proportionate legs and thighs showed him as a giant among pygmies.

There was however, something ungainly in his huge frame and more of awkwardness than symmetry in his configuration. Brassey, although less, was still "a man for a' that" and if not in juxtaposition with such a Goliath would have been regarded as an excellent specimen of the Grenadier fraternity. His figure was muscular and his limbs well knit, exhibiting appearances of strength and vigour not to be despised, while his mug displayed fearless determination.

Of the two, Caunt looked by far the more formidable. Thanks mainly to Peter Crawley who had got him into such perfect condition, there did not seem to be a pound of superfluous flesh upon his enormous figure.

The preliminaries having been completed, at twenty-five minutes after nine the men stepped up to the scratch and with the rain steadily falling upon their naked torsos, 'business' commenced.

Beyond the privileged stood rows of perpendicular spectators and behind them again were the carriages and other vehicles, covered with not less anxious gazers.

THE FIGHT

Round 1:
No sooner had the seconds retired to their corners, on leaving the men at the scratch, than Caunt rushed to his man and threw out his arms, left and right, with the quickness and vigour of a just-started windmill; his kind intentions were however, evaded and he missed his blows, especially a terrific upper-cut with his right which, had it reached its destination, would have "told a tale". Brassey in like manner was wild and missed his blows, but finding Caunt closing upon him, he hit up with his right and on closing instantly went down.

Round 2:
Caunt again hit out left and right, but without precision. He made his right slightly on Brassey's nob[9], when the latter rattled in left and right, like Caunt, missing and again went down. It was pretty obvious that Brassey was fearful of Caunt's favourite hug of Ursa Major[10] and had made up his mind to the falling system, which however obnoxious to the spectators, was evidently his only safe game.

As they came up for the second bout it was evident that the Nottingham man meant playing a forcing game, and Brassey seemed to have no desire to meet him at too close quarters. In fact, at the commencement he seemed to be afraid of getting near to the Herculean frame and went down for the second time without much provocation, being hissed by some of the spectators.

Round 3:
"Steady", cried Dick, "and hit straight". Caunt led off right and left and succeeded in planting his left on Brassey's forehead, but he had it in return. Brassey got to him and delivered a tremendous left-hander on his cheek and was as quick with his right on his nozzle[11]; the claret flew in abundance and the Big 'Un was posed. He hit out wild, left and right and missed, while Brassey got down. (Loud cheers for Brassey. The spectators were electrified by the effect of these blows. A gaping wound ornamented Caunt's right cheek and his nose emitted the purple fluid, which Dick quickly mopped up with his sponge). This decided the first event - first blood for Brassey.

---

[9] The head

[10] A constellation containing the seven stars that form the Great Bear.

[11] The nose

Round 4:
Caunt came up by no means improved in beauty. He led off as before, wild left and right; but his deliveries wanted precision. Brassey fought with him, but like sticks in an Irish row, their arms were the only receivers and little mischief was done. Brassey got down grinning.

Just as the men came up for the fourth round John Gully, who was standing close to the ropes, turned round to a knot of noblemen and gentlemen who were wagering on the fight and said, "I will back Brassey for any part of a thousand." The words were scarcely out of his mouth before old Ben Butler, Caunt's uncle and principal backer, held up his hand and shouted "I'll gi' 'ee a hundred, Muster Gully." "All right," said the veteran gladiator, "You're on." But no one else for the moment seemed inclined to back the Big 'Un. And when Caunt appeared at the scratch, the state of his features was not such as to inspire his friends with confidence. The blood was still welling from his nose and from a deep gash in his cheek and the severity of Brassey's hitting was thus palpably proved. Ben, too, was very unsteady; he led off wildly with right and left and seemed to let fly at random. Brassey was not much better and the blows of both fell on one another's arms and shoulders, doing no mischief whatsoever. When the Yorkshireman, however, found Ben pressing him too close he went down "grinning horribly a ghastly smile" as he did so.

Rounds 5 to 12:
The next eight rounds were a very poor exhibition of fighting and old stagers present drew very uncomplimentary comparisons between the performances of these two hulking pretenders and that of such men as Spring, or Gully, or Cribb, or Bill Neate, or Big Brown of Bridgnorth. Caunt sent in some fearful blows, no doubt any one of which, had it gone home, would have been sufficient to knock his man out of time but then he invariably missed - his great shoulder of mutton fist time after time flew harmlessly over Brassey's shoulder. The Yorkshireman however, was not much more successful. Now and then he popped in a straight one with his left, but with none of the stinging severity of the two scorchers he had landed in the third round and whenever Caunt rushed at him he dropped. On seeing this, Ben would stand astride over him, pointing at him with derision and contempt. Once or twice Brassey went down so quickly that Ben had the greatest difficulty to avoid treading on his prostrate foe. Many men would have lost their temper at such shifty and unmanly tactics, but Ben was not easily put out and bore the trying conduct of his adversary with imperturbable phlegm. What astonished the spectators most however, was the fact that when this Herculean giant did get

home a blow it appeared to have very little effect upon Brassey. Ben's heaviest blows all missed their mark and at the close of the twelfth round neither man was any more punished than at the end of the third.

Caunt planted his left on Brassey's eye, but missed his right which, had it reached it destination, would have been a poser. It went over Brassey's shoulder. Brassey, finding he could not well stand the overwhelming rush of his antagonist, got down.

Round 6:
Brassey popped in his left and escaping the visitation of Caunt's left and right pursued his tumbling system, while Caunt laughed and pointed at him with contempt.

Round 7:
Caunt, more successful, caught Brassey left and right on the nob, when Brassey went down, but Caunt's blows did not seem to tell.

Round 8:
Caunt delivered his left and right, but so wildly as to be ineffective and Brassey went down, throwing up his legs and knees in the rebound.

Round 9:
Caunt, as usual, opened the ball with a wild rush right and left, catching Brassey on the forehead with his right. Brassey hit left and right, but was stopped and went down, Caunt with difficulty escaping treading on him as he stepped over him.

Rounds 10 to 12:
All of the same character, Caunt doing no great execution and Brassey invariably getting down.

Round 13:
Caunt hit out of distance with his right, when Brassey caught him on the smeller with his left, again drawing his cork. Caunt, stung, hit out heavily with his right and caught Brassey on the back of the ear. Brassey went down.

Round 14:
Caunt, the first to fight, planted his right on Brassey's left eye; Brassey fell. (First knockdown blow claimed, but doubtful, as the ground became inconveniently slippery).

Round 15:
Caunt missed one of his tremendous right-hand lunges and Brassey went down.

Round 16:
Caunt dropped heavily with his right on Brassey's ribs, who fought wildly, but again caught Caunt with the left on his damaged cheek; more blood and Brassey down.

Round 17:
Brassey in with his right on Caunt's ogle[12] and went down.

Round 18:
Caunt in his wild rush, hit Brassey left and right on the pimple[13] and on his going down, as he stepped over him, scraped his forehead with his shoe, peeling off a trifle of the bark.

Round 19:
Caunt, more steady, planted his left on Brassey's dexter peeper[14] and hit him clear down with his right (First knockdown blow unequivocally declared for Caunt).

Round 20:
Caunt delivered his left heavily on Brassey's snout; and his right on the side of his head. Brassey made play, but missed and went down. On being lifted on his second's knee, he bled from mouth and nose.

(The friends of Caunt, who had been silent up to this, regarding the issue of the battle anything but certain, now again opened their potato traps and offered 2 to 1 which was taken).

---

[12] The eye
[13] The head
[14] The right eye

Round 21:
Caunt delivered another heavy body blow with his right, which made a resounding echo. Brassey rushed to a close and clung with his legs around Caunt's thighs. Caunt tried to hold him up with his left while he hit with his right, but he found this impossible and flung him down with contempt. It was here clear that if once Brassey suffered himself to be grasped in a punishable position by his opponent it would be all over.

Rounds 22 to 25:
These rounds were all pretty much in the same style - the hitting wild and ineffective, Brassey either clinging to his man or throwing himself down.

Round 26:
Another heavy blow on the ribs from Caunt's right told smartly on Brassey's corporation. Brassey attempted to close, but Caunt threw him heavily with his head on the ground.

Rounds 27 to 29:
Not much done, Brassey going down every round, after slight and wild exchanges.

Round 30:
Caunt hit Brassey down with one of his swinging right-handed hits on the side of his head, which made his left eye twinkle again (3 to 1 offered and taken on Caunt).

Rounds 31 to 33:
In the next three rounds there were some heavy exchanges left and right, but Brassey pursued his falling tactics.

Round 34:
Tremendous counter-hitting with the right and equally heavy exchanges with the left. Both down on their knees, from the stunning severity of the deliveries. (Caunt's beauty improving. A splendid likeness of the "Saracen's Head" without his wig).

Round 35:
Again did Caunt nail his man on the nose with his left and the claret came forth freely.

Rounds 36 to 54:
During these rounds there were some heavy exchanges left and right. To all appearance, the punishment was most severe on Caunt's face, whose left cheek was cut, as well as his right, but the heavy deliveries on the left side of Brassey's head as well as his ribs, had evidently weakened him, although he still came up as game as a pebble. In his frequent falls, Caunt occasionally could not avoid falling on him and his weight was no trifling addition to his other punishment. It is but just to state however, that Caunt fought in a fair and manly style and avoided everything like unfair advantage.

Round 55:
In the 55th round the ground became so muddy that the men, from fighting in the centre of the ring, could scarcely keep their legs and Brassey went down without a blow. This was claimed, but rejected by the referee, who cautioned him however, against giving such another chance away.

Round 56:
Caunt planted his left heavily on Brassey's winker, but Brassey in return, hit him on the jaw with his right and making up his mind for further mischief, repeated the blow with terrific effect a little below the same spot, Caunt countering at the same moment and with the same hand. The collision was dreadful - both fell in opposite directions - Caunt as if shot by a twenty-four pounder and Brassey all abroad.

Here was a decided change; Caunt was evidently unconscious and was with difficulty held on his second's knee. His head rolled like a turtle in convulsions. Curtis, however, steadied his tremulous pimple, administered a slight dash of water and on "Time" being called he was enabled to go to the scratch, but with such groggy indications that it is doubtful whether he knew if he was on his head or his heels.

Round 57:
Brassey now endeavoured to improve his advantage, but instead of steadily waiting to give his man the coup de grace, he rushed in and bored Caunt through the ropes and he fell on his back while the force of Brassey's fall on him was stayed by his own chin being caught by the upper rope, on which he hung for a moment.

Round 58:
Caunt recovered a little, but Brassey again rushed in, hitting left and right and in the struggle both went down, Brassey uppermost.

Round 59:
Caunt steadied himself and went in to fight. Some heavy exchanges followed and Brassey went down, but Caunt was far from firm on his pins. It was now seen that Caunt's right hand, from its repeated visit to Brassey's head and ribs, was much swollen; his left too, showed the effects of repeated contact with the physog[15] of his antagonist. This, in the following rounds, led to a good deal of contention, on the ground that Caunt had unfair substances in his hand; but he showed it was only paper and threw it away, although entitled to the use of any soft material to steady his grasp.

Rounds 60 to 90:
The rounds which followed, to the 90th, offered but little variety; both men became gradually exhausted and it required all the care and encouragement of their partisans to rouse them to action. Each was assured that victory smiled upon him and that it only required another effort to make all safe. Brassey came up manfully round after round; but although he occasionally stopped and hit, the pops of his opponent, who now and then saved him the trouble of falling by hitting him down, told with increasing effect. Caunt repeatedly tried to hold him in the closes, with the view of fibbing; but Brassey was too leery and got down without this additional proof of kind intention. In some of his tumbles however, Caunt fell heavily on him and once more, in trying to evade him, scraped his foot on his nose, a casualty almost unavoidable from his sudden prostrations.

The weakness of Brassey gradually increased, whilst Caunt evidently got stronger on his legs; and although his right hand was gone, he continued to hit with it. He was entreated to use his left, which he did three times in succession in one round on Brassey's muzzle[16], till he dropped him. Such was the prejudice in favour of Brassey however, from the vigour with which he occasionally rallied, that it was still hoped he might make a turn in his favour and if encouraging shouts would have effected that object, he was not without

---

[15] The face
[16] The mouth

stentorian[17] friends. Caunt too, had his anxious attendant and all that cheering could do to rouse his spirits was heartily afforded him.

Rounds 90 to 100:
From the 90th to the 100th round poor Brassey came up weak on his legs and either fell or was hit down, but to the last made a manly struggle against superior strength and weight. In the 100th round Broome said he should fight no more and Crawley stepped into the ring to claim the battle; he was however, called out and Brassey came up once more, but he was incapable of prolonged exertion and being hit down with a right-handed smack on the head, he reluctantly submitted to the calls of his friends to give in and all was over. Caunt was proclaimed the conqueror, after fighting one hundred and one rounds, in one hour and thirty minutes. In ninety minutes one hundred rounds were fought, deducting the half minute time, often prolonged to nearly a minute by mutual delay, in coming to the "scratch" when "time" was called; therefore, the average time occupied by each round did not much exceed twenty seconds.

Caunt was invariably the first to fight, but led off with nothing like precision, repeatedly missing his blows and upper cuts, many of which, had they told, might have been conclusive. Brassey seemed to be fully aware of this mode of assault and generally waited till he got within Caunt's guard and thus succeeded in administering heavy punishment. This point once gained he lost no time in getting down, feeling quite confident, that in close contact he would not have had a chance. This, although far from a popular mode of contest, is certainly excusable considering the inequality of the men in height and weight and the only surprise is that the lesser man should have endured so much before he cried "enough". The repeated visitations to his ribs from Caunt's right, or "sledge-hammer", were searching in the extreme and led to the belief that three of his ribs had been broken, although subsequent examination proved that he was only labouring under the effects of severe contusions and inward bruises. In like manner the right-handed deliveries behind his left ear, on the ear itself and on the left eye and jaw, as well as the left-handed jabs, were so far from jocular that it was not surprising that the smiling face had ceased to be displayed on his "dial" and when to these visitations are added his repeated falls, with the weight of Caunt occasionally added to his own and this in such rapid succession, the only surprise is he should have held out so long.

---

[17] People with powerful voices

Caunt in his modus operandi evinced a said ignorance of the art. Like the yokels of old before the principles of mechanism were discovered, he has to learn the proper application of his strength, of which, did he possess the requisite knowledge, he might bid defiance not only to such a man as Brassey, but even to the caperings of an avalanche. He is not, like most men of his size, slow - on the contrary, he is too quick; and for want of judicious deliberation, like a runaway steam-engine without a controlling engineer, he over-shoots his mark. This, if it be possible, he ought to correct and while he husbands his strength, where he does apply it, he should measure not only his distance but the tactics of his opponent. Had he waited for his man, instead of leading off with a rush, he must have brought Brassey down every round, for nothing could resist the force of his heavy metal if properly applied. Strange as it may appear on examining both men on Wednesday morning, the punishment on the part of Caunt was greater than that of Brassey and viewing both frontispieces and saying, "Look on this picture and on this", our opinion would have been, "Caunt has received the greater and more effective punishment". Added to this, his hands and especially, the right were essentially hors de combat, while Brassey's were uninjured. Upon the whole, therefore, although Caunt is the victor and entitled to top praise, Brassey, as the vanquished, deserves almost an equal degree or credit, if not of profit. That this is the feeling of others was demonstrated at Newmarket after the battle, for there was not only £30 collected for him by voluntary contributions, but a promise of still more liberal consideration was held out and in the end fulfilled.

On the Monday following the fight, at Peter Crawley's Queen's Head and French Horn in Smithfield, the battle money was paid over to Caunt, in the presence of an overflowing muster of the patrons of British boxing. Brassey was present and confessed himself fairly conquered. A subscription was made to console him for his honourable defeat and £40 presented to him as a reward for his valiant conduct, some merriment being excited by one of the donations being announced as from "the parson of Cheveley".

Caunt, in a short speech, stated that he once again claimed the "Championship of England" and was ready to make, then and there, a match for £100 a side with any man, to fight within fifty miles of London.

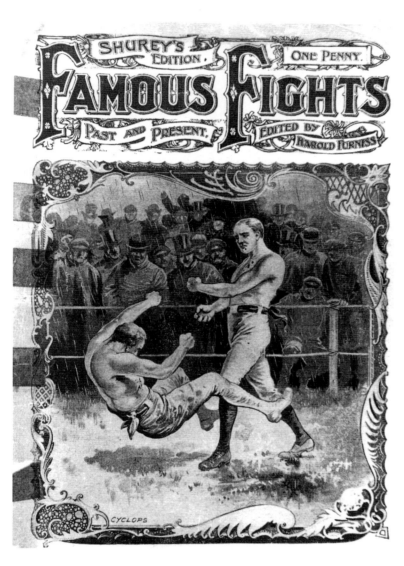

Ben Caunt and Brassey

What follows next are extracts from the recollections of one Baron Brampton travelling to Newmarket for the races with his friend Charley Wright which give an interesting insight of the times:

"An interesting episode interrupted our journey to the Heath. To our surprise and to our delight, there was to be an important meeting of the Fancy to witness a great prize-fight between Jack Brassey and Ben Caunt.

Ben Caunt was the greatest prize-fighter, both in stature and bulk, as well as in strength, I ever saw. He looked what he was - then or soon after - the champion of the world.

Brassey, too, was well made and seemed every bit the man to meet Caunt. The two, indeed, were equally well made in form and shape and as smooth cut as marble statues when they stripped for action.

It was different weather from that the Fancy enjoyed in the early morning, for the rain was now pouring down in torrents and we had a drive of no less than fifteen miles before us to the scene of action. Vehicles were few and horses fewer. Nothing was to be had for love or money, as it seemed. But there was at last found one man who, if he had little love for the Prize Ring, had much reverence for the golden coin that supported it. He was a Quaker. He had an old gig and, I think, a still older horse, both of which I hired for the journey. The Quaker, of course, pretending that he had no idea of any meeting of the Fancy whatever. Nor do I suppose he would know what that term implied.

If ever any man in the world did what young men are always told by good people to do namely, to persevere, I am sure we did, Charley and I, with the Quaker's horse. Whether he suspected the mission on which we were bent, or was considering the danger of such a scene to his morals, I could not ascertain, but never did any animal show a greater reluctance to go anywhere except to his quiet home.

Your happiness at these great gatherings depended entirely upon the distance or proximity of the police. If they were pretty near, the landlord of the inn would hesitate about serving you and if he did, would charge a far higher price in consequence of the supposed increased risk. He would never encourage a breach of the peace in defiance of the county magistrates, who were the authority to renew his licence at Brewster Sessions. So much, then, if the officers of justice were near.

If they happened to be absent which, as I have said occasionally occurred when a big thing was to come off there was then a dominant feeling of social equality which you could never see manifested so strongly in any other place. A gentleman would think nothing of putting his fingers into your pockets and abstracting your money and if you had the hardihood to resent the intrusion, would think less of putting his fist into your eyes.

Thus we set out for the rendezvous. Charley soon discovered that our steed was not accustomed to the whip, for instead of urging him forward it produced the contrary effect. However, we got along by slow degrees and when we came up with the crowd - oh!

Such a scene I had never witnessed in my life, nor could have conceived it possible anywhere on this earth or anywhere out of that abyss the full description of which you will find in Paradise Lost.

It was a procession of the blackguardism of all ages and of all countries under heaven. The sexes were apparently in equal numbers and unequal degrees of ugliness and ferocity: There were faces flat for want of noses and mouths ghastly for want of teeth; faces scarred, bruised, battered into every shape but what might be called human. There were fighting-men of every species and variety - men whose profession it was to fight and others whose brutal nature it was; there were women fighters, too, more deadly and dangerous than the men, because they added cruelty to their ferocity. Innumerable women there were who had lost the very nature of womanhood and whose mouths were the mere outlet of oaths and filthy language. Their shrill clamours deafened our ears and subdued the deep voices of the men, whom they chaffed, reviled, shrieked at, yelled at and swore at by way of fun.

Amidst this turbulent rabble rode several members of the peerage and even Ministerial supporters of the 'noble art,' exchanging with the low wretches I have mentioned a word or two of chaff or an occasional laugh at the grotesque wit and humour which are never absent from an English crowd.

Every face was now white with excitement, except the faces of the combatants. They were firm set as iron itself. Trained to physical endurance, they were equally so in nerve and coolness of temperament and could not have seemed more excited than if they were going to dinner instead of to one of the most terrible encounters I ever witnessed.

We had been advised to take our cushions from the gig to sit upon, because the straw round the ring was soddened with the heavy rains and I need not say we found it was a very wise precaution. The straw had been placed round the ring for the benefit of the elite, who occupied front seats.

The fight now began and, I must repeat, I never saw anything like it. Both pugilists were of the heaviest fighting weights. Caunt was a real giant, ugly as could be by the frequent batterings he had received in the face. His head was like a bull-dog's and so was his courage, whilst his strength must have been that of a very Samson; but if it was, it did not reside in his hair, for that was short and close as a mouse's back.

At first I thought Brassey had the best of it - he was more active, being less ponderous and landed some very ugly ones, cutting right into the flesh, although Caunt did not appear to mind it in the least. Brassey, however, did not follow up his advantage as I thought he ought to have done and in my opinion dreaded the enormous power and force of his opponent in the event of his 'getting home.'

With the usual fluctuations of a great battle, the contest went on until nearly a hundred rounds were fought, lasting as many minutes, but no decisive effect was as yet observable. After this, however, Brassey could not come up to time. The event, therefore, was declared in Caunt's favour and his opponent was carried off the field on a hurdle into the public-house, where I afterwards saw him in bed.

Thus terminated the great fight of the day, but not thus my day's adventures.

Alas! our respectability was gone - I mean the gig.

In vindication of the wisdom and foresight of Charley and myself, I should like to mention that we had entrusted that valuable evidence of our status to the keeping of a worthy stranger dressed in an old red jacket and a pair of corduroy trousers fastened with a wisp of hay below the knees.

When we arrived at the spot where he promised to wait our coming, he was gone, the horse and gig too; nor could any inquiries ascertain their whereabouts."

Chapter 5

BEN FIGHTS WARD FOR THE CHAMPIONSHIP

(1840)

Towards the end of 1840, it was difficult to decide who was entitled to call himself Champion of England. Jem Ward had presented a belt to Bendigo and appointed him his successor to the title, which he had held for some fourteen years. The presentation took place on February 12th, 1839.

Deaf Burke had challenged Ward and Bendigo had beaten the Deaf 'Un, so perhaps Bendigo had as much right or more to the title than anybody else did at the time. About a year after this, in March 1840, Bendigo met with a serious accident which left him unable to fight and completely out of the running, leaving the Championship wide open once more. The Fancy looked around for the coming man and the most likely one they found was the gigantic Ben Caunt, who had just managed to defeat Brassey by the skin of his teeth. Indeed, Ben himself always said that beating Brassey was the toughest bit of work he ever accomplished.

Following this victory Ben had the stakes presented to him at Peter Crawley's house, the Queen's Head and French Horn, in Duke Street Smithfield, at which a tremendous muster of the Fancy attended. In returning thanks to his friends, Caunt stated that he claimed the Championship and although Nick Ward had challenged him to contest the title, Ben feared that it was all bounce and that the brother of the ex-Champion was not inclined to meet him. This came to Jem's ears and he at once wrote the following letter to the leading sporting journals of the day:

"The friends of Nick Ward have consulted and consider (as his efforts in the Prize Ring have been few and as you, whose judgement, from long experience, is entitled to great weight, have expressed an opinion that Nick Ward never would be a first-rate man), that Caunt, who lays claim to the Championship, should, as a set-off to his superiority of weight and position, give odds to make a match. Nick Ward, with out bouncing, is willing to fight Caunt if he will deposit £150 to Ward's £100.
"JAMES WARD
"Star Hotel, Williamson Square, Liverpool.
"November 12th, 1840"

This letter created no small comment in sporting circles. Caunt made no direct reply, but on the Thursday following the publication of the letter he took a benefit at the Bloomsbury Assembly Rooms and after the boxing was over there were two important matters to announce. One was that our Most Gracious Majesty the Queen had been safely delivered of a daughter (Princess Victoria born on November 21st) and three hearty cheers were given by those who were in the crowded house. Then came a statement by Young Dutch Sam, who said that he was empowered to post a 'fiver' on behalf of Nick Ward, towards a match for £100 with Caunt. This was then and there accepted and covered by Big Ben, the money being handed over to Tom Spring, on the understanding that the men were to meet on Tuesday, December 8th and sign articles to fight.

The appointment was kept; Peter Crawley signed for Caunt and Young Sam for Ward, agreeing to fight a fair stand-up fight in a twenty-four foot ring, half-minute time, within sixty miles of London, on Tuesday, February 2nd, 1841, for £100 a side, according to the provisions of the rules.

The following Articles of Agreement were entered into this 8th day of December 1840, between Benjamin Caunt and Nicholas Ward:

The said Ben Caunt agrees to fight the said Nick Ward, a fair stand-up fight, in a four and twenty foot roped ring, half minute time, within sixty miles of London, on Tuesday, the 2nd of February, 1841, for £100 a side, according to the provisions of the new rules. In pursuance of this agreement, £20 a side are now deposited; a second deposit of £10 a side to be made on Thursday, the 17th of December, at Young Dutch Sam's; a third deposit of £10 a side on Monday, the 21st of December, at Peter Crawley's; a fourth deposit of £10 a side, on Thursday, the 31st of December, at Jem Ward's, Liverpool; a fifth deposit of £10 a side, on Friday, the 8th of January, 1841, at Owen Swift's; a sixth deposit of £10 a side, on Thursday, the 14th of January, at Young Dutch Sam's; a seventh deposit of £10 a side, on Monday, the 18th of January, at Peter Crawley's; and the eighth and last deposit of £10 a side, on Thursday, the 28th of January, at the same house: the said deposits to be made between the hours of eight and ten in the evening, or the party failing to forfeit the money down. The choice of place to be decided at the last deposit by toss. The men to be in the ring between the hours of twelve and one o'clock, or the party absent to forfeit the battle-money, unless an earlier hour shall be mutually agreed upon at the last deposit, to which hour the same forfeiture shall be applicable. Two umpires and a referee are to be chosen on the ground. In case of dispute the decision of the latter to be conclusive. Should magisterial interference take place, the stakeholder to name the next time and place of meeting, if possible on the same day. The use of resin or other powder to the hands during the battle to be considered foul and the money not to be given up till fairly won or lost by a fight.

Signed for Caunt - PETER CRAWLEY.
Signed for Ward - SAMUEL EVANS.

Nicholas Ward, the brother of the ex-Champion Jem (James) was born on April 1st, 1813, at St George's-in-the East and, like his two brothers John and James and their father, followed the occupation of a coal-whipper[18], which undoubtedly had much to do with the development of their muscles. They inherited their fighting proclivities, like Bendigo, from their mother, for by all accounts she was a perfect Amazon and was very smart with her fists.

Nick was some thirteen years younger than his brother Jem, but was quite as powerful as that phenomenon, even when the latter was at his best. Furthermore he was, in many people's opinion, quite as clever and as quick as lightning, besides being a tremendously hard hitter. There was one fault, however, he possessed and that was the lack of that quality which is more essential than anything else in the making of a pugilist. Nick Ward had a heart no bigger than a chicken's and could not stand being hit. Unlike his brother Jem, directly he received punishment it was all over. Yet he could summon courage enough to engage in battle with the best of them. And then, as the following performances will show, he proved on several occasions to be a most arrant coward and his career was by no means a brilliant one.

He commenced by defeating Harry Lockyer, of Kent, on February 24th, 1835.

He then came out in his true colours, by sneaking out of a match with Young Molyneaux, he having procured his own arrest on the day before the fight was arranged to come off.

He again showed the white feather when he met Sam Sutton during the Derby week of 1836, surrendering in the most ignominious and dastardly manner, when all thought he was winning in the easiest possible manner, simply because Sutton struck him a violent blow on the nose. One writer at the time

---

[18] One who unloads coal from a ship's hold.

declared that the sight and smell of his own blood turned him sick, for nothing would induce him to stand up before Sutton after the receipt of that blow. In fact, he openly declared that he was not cut out for a fighting man. Still his brother and friends were still able to persuade him to enter the lists. Sutton was forever chaffing Nick Ward and at length Nick could stand it no longer and they were matched to fight a second time for £50 a side on March 27th, 1838. But this came to nothing, for Sam was captured by the police on the morning of the battle and Ward was chased for thirty miles by the constables, who, however, did not succeed in arresting him.

His next attempt was in his long and shifty fight with Jem Bailey, which took place on October 18th, 1839, when Nick Ward had the battle given to him through his adversary striking a foul blow. Then a second match was made but Nick flunked it again and declared that he was 'too unwell' to enter the arena and so he forfeited.

Although this does not sound like the record of a great champion his supporters thought him good enough to warrant him wearing the belt, which had been buckled around his brother's waist. That he must have been a good man is proved by the fact that he defeated Deaf Burke, that game, scientific and hard-hitting fighter, who had carried everything before him until he was defeated by Bendigo. Having said that, Burke's days were coming to an end when he met Nick and he was suffering from lameness, which prevented him from following his lively antagonist about the ring. Nobody could fight better than Ward if he found it was all going his way and in this battle the poor old Deaf 'Un was soon winded and exhausted, when Nick went for him in a most unmerciful manner, the Deaf 'Un being quite over matched. This was the most creditable of all Ward's performances and he was so elated that he determined to make a bid for the Championship. That he had a good claim to it there could be no doubt, for he had beaten Burke, who stood next to Bendigo for the coveted honours. There was only Caunt to defeat, who had beaten Bendigo.

On Tuesday the 2nd of February then, this anxiously anticipated meeting took place, but resulted in a manner anything but satisfactory to the admirers of manly pugilism.

Nick had been staying with his brother Jem at Liverpool and there remained until the second week in December, when he went off to the Hare and Hounds, West Derby, with Peter Taylor to look after him. There he was joined

James Burke – The Deaf 'Un

by an American bruiser of some notoriety who had just come to this country, known as Yankee Sullivan and who was engaged to fight Hammer Lane, of Birmingham, in the same ring in which Nick Ward and Ben Caunt were to figure. Peter Taylor had both men in hand, turning them out in splendid condition, for there wasn't a better trainer living than Peter.

Ben Caunt went off immediately the articles were signed, on tour, visiting Manchester, Bolton, Warrington and other northern towns, returning to London on December 17th, when Peter Crawley took Ben to Hatfield, near Barnet, where he went into strict training.

The last deposit for the match was duly made at Peter Crawley's and on that occasion, Thursday, January 28th Mr. Gervase Harker, of Stoneyford, who was Caunt's principal backer, won the toss for choice of battle-ground. He selected Andover Road Station, on the South Western (then known as the Southampton Railway). This necessitated a journey of no less a distance than two hundred and fifty miles for Nick Ward and his party. This was seen as most inconsiderate on the part of Mr. Harker because this decision did not reach them until the Saturday morning, leaving them little time to make their arrangements for so long a journey and get comfortably to the far off Hampshire.

On the Sunday morning, two days before the fight, Nick Ward accompanied by his brother Jem, Peter Taylor, Young Molyneaux, Mat Robinson, Yankee Sullivan and a number of friends and backers, set off from Liverpool. They did not arrive at their destination until the Monday morning, when they put up at the well known sporting house The Catherine Wheel in Andover.

Ben Caunt on the other hand had journeyed down much more comfortably from his training quarters with Hammer Lane departing on the Sunday and arriving the same evening. On arrival the pair put up at the Vine at Stockbridge about ten miles from the Winchester Station, where they were joined by a select circle of their backers and friends.

On the Monday, sportsmen arrived at Andover in their hundreds and so great was the run upon the inns that many found it necessary to go on to Winchester, finding accommodation at the Royal, the Swan, the Crown and other hostelries. The owners of the houses of entertainment in the neighbourhood were understandably delighted.

Hammer Lane

When the two parties met there was a deal of ill feeling on the part of the Wardites, who had been brought such a distance and when it became known that the Hampshire constabulary were on the scent their rage knew no bounds.

The principal parties engaged met on the Monday evening at the Catherine Wheel to discuss what was to be done. Caunt's backers declared that it was for no purpose of inconveniencing Ward and his friends that they had selected Hampshire, but for the purpose of giving the sports there a treat, the latter having promised to pay handsomely toward the men's expenses. Still it seemed that there was no possibility of bringing the battle off there and they suggested a move into Wiltshire. The Wardites objected to this, as it would have brought the place outside the distance fixed upon by the articles. At length it was decided to journey into Berkshire and Cookham Common was fixed upon. This meant a journey of some fourteen miles and so those who had to travel on foot had a nice journey before them.

Fortunately, Tuesday, the day of the fight, was fine and frosty. At half-past ten, the village of Sutton displayed a dense congregation of all classes, from the high-titled nob to the wooden-soled chaw-bacon[19]. Carriages of all sorts, from Winchester, Andover, Stockbridge, Odiham and all the surrounding post-towns, as well as from London and elsewhere, were huddled together in tangled confusion, anxiously waiting to receive the authorised "office" as to the road they should take. Among these the Commissary, in a light chaise cart, with the indispensable material of his calling, occupied a prominent position, while the belligerents in their respective drags patiently waited the order for advance. Amidst the turmoil, the superintendent and the inspectors of the rural police, attended by a number of constables, some on horseback and some in chaise carts were preparing to do their duty and to see the expectant multitude fairly out of their jurisdiction.

The throng included some swell sportsmen including the Earl of Portsmouth, who had driven with some friends from his beautiful seat of Hurstbourne Park. Mr. John Portal Brydges had come from the Freefolk Paper Mills near Whitchurch where the paper for bank notes had been manufactured since the time of George I. Mr. William Portal, of Laverstock was also there and a host of Hampshire squires, gentlemen and farmers.

---

[19] A yokel

The journey was up hill and down dale and a very tiresome route. Many incidents and accidents happened on the road, including the break down of the gig chartered by Johnny Hannan, who had to be transferred to the drag upon which Ben Caunt was being conveyed to the battle-field.

At Whitchurch the inhabitants were rather astonished at the sudden incursion of the cavalcade. Here there was a general halt for refreshment for man and beast and most ominously, the carriage in which Hammer Lane was placed broke down, an unfortunate fracture which was imitated by many other vehicles, many of which had been brought out of retirement for this particular occasion.

A further stop was enjoyed at Kings Clere and many of the jaded horses were for a time placed in stables, while the bonifaces[20] received ample proofs of the beneficial effects resulting to the human appetite when whetted against the rough edge of a hard frost and a bracing atmosphere.

It was now ascertained that the 'Promised Land' was within three miles of the village and the Commissary was sent forward to make the necessary preparations for action. The horses of the police, sharing the fate of their companions, were so knocked up that their masters determined to perform the rest of their journey to the verge of the county on foot. In half an hour the general body made their final move and, crossing the river Enborne, at last made their exit from the inhospitable county of Hants and luckily sustained no further impediment. They reached the battlefield on Crookham Common about half-past three, quickly forming a spacious circle round the ring, which had been admirably prepared by the commissariat department. The ground had a thin covering of snow and was bone hard from the intensity of the frost while a biting breeze came from the east. The assemblage, if not as numerous as might have been anticipated had not the move taken place, was in the honest sense of the word respectable and many persons of bona fide distinction, both as to rank and station in society, studded the lively circle.

The choosing of the umpires was straightforward. The difficulty of selecting a referee presented more of a problem and was eventually solved but only after considerable arguments.

---

[20] Inn keepers

All being now prepared for combat, the men entered the ring, greeted by the cheers of their friends. The picture of Caunt as he stood in the ring, his colossal figure and great, clumsy limbs being in strange contrast to Nick Ward's beautifully symmetrical frame, with its grand deep chest and finely shaped arms. He was a fine man standing 6ft and weighing 12st 10lbs. But at the onset Nick showed that he was afraid of his opponent. Caunt came forward attended by Tass Parker and Johnny Broome, all sporting their - "yellow men" while Nick Ward made his bow under the friendly introduction of Dick Curtis and Harry Holt, each of whom displayed a fogle[21] of blue and white spots. The men instantly advanced and shook hands with apparent good-humour. Ward looked rather serious, while Caunt exhibited a nonchalance and gaiety, which proved that he regarded the coming engagement with anything but personal apprehension. The betting round the ring at this moment was 5 to 4 on Caunt, with ready takers and with the preliminaries having been fully adjusted, the joust commenced.

THE FIGHT

Round 1:
On taking up their positions, the scientific manner in which Ward presented himself, with his arms well up, prepared to stop with his right and shoot with his left, gave evident tokens of his being an accomplished member of the scientific school. Caunt also held his arms well up, albeit with a degree of awkwardness, but he had evidently made up his mind to lose no time in commencing operations and he advanced upon his man, but Ward flinched and drew back step by step as the bigger man advanced. The latter at length lashed out, but was cleverly stopped by Nick, who returned one, two on the face but there was little power in the blows and Ben grinned at his opponent and made another dash. A smart rally ensued with Ward's left creating a blushing tinge on the Big 'Un's cheek, but both men were hurried with Caunt too eager to get home and Ward too anxious to get away - so the blows were dealt random and ill-aimed. The Big 'Un then tried to close, just managing to hold his opponent for a few seconds, but the latter cleverly slipped from his grasp and went down.

Round 2:
In the succeeding round Nick Ward dodged his adversary splendidly all over the ring, now and again getting in a stinging blow, but doing little damage.

---

[21] A silk handkerchief.

Caunt though, got wild at not being able to hit or grapple his foe partly due to the slippery state of the ground, as it was obvious that neither combatant could obtain firm footing partly due to his slippery opponent. It seemed that his temper was getting beyond his control, as it did in his battle with Bendigo. Ward's tricky tactics did not suit him and he showed unmistakable signs of rising wrath. Ward was encouraged by Dick Curtis to continue to irritate Ben who, mad with himself for missing, rushed in to close but Nick, as before, eluded his grasp and dropped. Then Caunt, when in his corner, was mercilessly heckled by Ward's friends. All this was done for a purpose.

Round 3:
Ward came up tentatively, prepared to either defend or attack. He waited for the attack, which was soon commenced by Caunt with vigorous but wild determination. He stopped left and right, but in his returns was short, his attacks not reaching their intended point of contact. Both in fact missed their blows and no real mischief was done. Caunt rushed to a close, but Ward, still resolved to foil the grappling propensity of his opponent, slipped down.

Round 4:
In the fourth round there were heavy exchanges left and right, in which Caunt caught a stinger on the forehead and the nose, from which blood was drawn, Caunt countered and caught Ward a crack on the nob with his right. Ben got more and more savage and lost control of himself and became even more wild and awkward in his mode of attack. Had the other man been real grit he could have done considerable damage to his colossal opponent. But he was not and took more care to keep himself out of harm's way than to administer punishment. In the close Caunt caught Ward in his arms, but he again went down.

Round 5:
Caunt tried a feint to draw his man, but Nick was too wary. He preserved his own position, evidently determined to nail his man with the left on coming in. Caunt, impatient, hit out wildly with left and right but Nick broke ground and got away. On again getting to work Nick planted his left on Caunt's eye and slight exchanges followed, but no serious impression was made and Ward's left passed over Caunt's shoulder. During this round Caunt's deliveries carried neither force nor accuracy and because of this Ward was getting nearer his man and succeeded in planting a rap on his proboscis[22]. Caunt instantly seized

---

[22] Nose

him in his arms and was about to vent his frustration on him when Ward endeavoured to get down, but the Big 'Un held him too firmly and fell heavily upon him.

Round 6:
On coming up Caunt exhibited symptoms of visitations to his nose and eye, as well as to his forehead, but still no material damage had been affected. Ward led off with his left, but the hit was short and was attended with little effect. Caunt again closed, determined to give his man the benefit of one of his Nottinghamshire hugs, but Ward frustrated his intention by dropping on his knees. At the same moment Caunt, determined to give him a compliment as he fell, let fly his right, which did not reach its destination (Ward's lug) till Ward's knees had actually reached the ground. There was an immediate cry of "Foul" and the partisans of Ward, as well as his second, rushed to the referee to claim the battle. This was decidedly in opposition to the New Rules, which prescribe that *'all such appeals shall be made to the umpires and by them to the referee and that no other person whatever shall presume to interfere'*. Amid the turmoil and confusion the referee remained silent until the umpires declared they disagreed and when the question was then put to him deliberately pronounced "Fair," believing, as he said he did, that the blow was unintentional and had commenced its flight before Ward was actually on the ground. All cavil was now at an end and the fight proceeded; the friends of Caunt earnestly entreating that he would be cautious of what he was about and be particularly careful in avoiding the repetition of the blow, which the falling system of Ward might unintentionally lead him to administer.

Round 7:
Caunt tried for a close but was warmly peppered on the eyes and nose and then, trying again and getting Nick in his grasp, the latter frustrated his intention by dropping on his knees. Mad at finding his foe slipping from his grasp, Ben let go his hold and raising his ponderous fist, let drive at Nick's head, catching him on the ear, after his knees had touched the ground. "Foul", "Foul", was the cry and according to the accents the confusion beggars description. The tumult which ensued was appalling and Ward's friends threatened to lynch Mr. Bailey, the referee, if that gentleman did not award the fight to their man. But the official was a man of nerve and courage and when he found that the umpires disagreed, he said in reply to this question, "Was it fair or foul, sir?" he replied, "I believe the blow was unintentional and I order the men to continue the fight."

Caunt came up as fresh as a sucking bull and pregnant with deeds of mischief. Ward waited for him steadily and let fly his left, catching Caunt slightly on the mug. Caunt hit wildly left and right, but missed. Caunt then closed, again catching Ward in his forceps. Ward however, renewed his dropping system and slipped from between his arms onto his knees, his hand up. With Ward in this position, evidently down, Caunt instantaneously drew back his right hand and hit him twice on the side of the head. The shout of "Foul" was immediately renewed with redoubled ardour and a simultaneous appeal was again made to the referee by some dozen or so persons who crowded round him and they were all vociferously demanding confirmation of their own impressions. This indecorous and disgraceful dictation was again manfully resisted by the referee who, waiting with firmness till calmness was restored, listened to the appeal from the proper authorities and pronounced the last blow to be foul observing that Ward was clearly down upon both knees when the blows were delivered. Shouts of congratulation forthwith hailed Ward as the conqueror, a result which filled him with delight and he quit the ring with joyous satisfaction, scarcely exhibiting a mark of the conflict in which he had been engaged. Indeed of punishment he did not afford a specimen worth mentioning. The fight lasted but twelve minutes and terminated at three minutes after four o'clock.

The backer of Caunt was naturally irritated at this disappointment of his hopes and sustained by the authority of an old ring-goer contended that the decision of the referee, however honourably given, was in opposition to the rules of the Prize Ring. The rules stated that it was necessary for the man to have his hand on the ground, as well as both knees, before a blow given could be pronounced foul. With this in mind he gave notice to the stakeholder not to part with the stake or the bets until the point was settled.

The referee said he had given his decision with perfect impartiality and he believed with perfect justice. In confirmation of which he turned to a copy of Fistiana, which he had in his possession and quoted from thence (page 29) the 7th of Broughton's Rules, which provides, "That no person is to hit his adversary when he is down, or seize him by the hair, the breeches or any part below the waist; a man on his knees to be reckoned down." He then quoted the 14th of the New Rules of the Prize Ring (page 65), which provides, in the same spirit, "That a blow struck when a man is thrown, or down, shall be deemed foul. That a man with one hand and one knee on the ground, or with both knees on the ground, shall be deemed down and a blow given in either of these positions shall be considered foul, providing always, that when in such position, the man so down shall not himself strike, or attempt to strike." The articles having been framed according to the New Rules, this reference must be conclusive.

However, it was contended that in the battle between Tom Belcher and Dutch Sam, the Pugilistic Club had decided that a blow given when a man was on his knees, with both hands up, was not foul. But, as there was no written record of this decision and as it is opposed both to Broughton's Rules and the New Rules, the argument can have no weight and the stakes, however easily and unsatisfactorily won, were of right given to Ward.

Ward, in purchasing this almost bloodless victory, did not add much to his reputation. That he was entitled to the reward of conquest cannot be denied; but the opportunities of testing his improved qualities and courage were so limited, that it would be worse than hypocrisy to say he offered any peculiar claims to high praise. That he was more scientific than his opponent cannot be doubted; but it must be admitted that on comparing his tactics with the steady and cutting precision of his brother Jem, he had yet much to learn. Many of his blows were short, while others, well-intentioned, missed their aim - a circumstance probably to be ascribed to the slippery state of the ground and the unsteady manoeuvres of his opponent. Regarding his courage, no particular exception can be taken, for although going down or trying to go down in every round is unsightly in the eyes of the spectators and has the semblance of being opposed to the commonplace notion of a fair stand-up fight yet, according to the 12th of the New Rules, it will be seen that such an expedient is allowable that rule provides "that it shall be a fair stand-up fight and if either man shall wilfully throw himself down without receiving a blow, he will be deemed to have lost the battle: but this rule shall not apply to a man who in a close slips down from the grasp of his opponent to avoid punishment." Here blows had been exchanged and Ward obviously slipped down to avoid the punishment that Caunt had determined to administer. Moreover, it was to avoid the hugging and being borne on to the ropes, which Ward evaded by slipping from the intended embrace. With regard to Caunt, the loss of the battle was attributed to his uncontrollable impetuosity. That he would have been defeated in fair fight by his accomplished antagonist is by no means a settled point, for although he showed marks of tapping, he was quite as fresh and vigorous as when he commenced and was quite as likely to win in the last as he was in the first round. However, he still had much to learn. He wanted steadiness and precision and the wildness with which he hit defeated his own object. He also had to learn to curb his impetuosity and preserve that presence of mind the absence of which so speedily led to the downfall of his hopes in this case. So persuaded was he that he could have won, that immediately after judgement had been given against him, he declared he would make a fresh match and post the whole hundred of his own money. It is singular that in his fights with Bendigo and Brassey he seldom lost a due command over his temper, although both these men pursued the same course of getting down as Ward. With regard to Brassey, his gift of punishment is far more severe than that of Ward, as the evidence of Caunt's carved frontispiece on the former occasion sufficiently testified. Here, once again, as so often was the case a poem or 'Chant of the Ring' was written to celebrate the fight.

NICK WARD AND CAUNT.

Hurrah for the Ring and the bunch of fives!
Like a giant refreshed the Ring revives,
It awakens again to vigorous life
To scare the assassin and crush the knife;

Then welcome to earth as the flowers in spring
Be the glory renew'd of the Boxing Ring.
And over each British boxer brave,
Long may the banner of fair play wave.

Let Puritan sour in accents shrill
Rave against Fistiana still,
And owl-faced beaks shake the nob and vow
To their fiat stern the Ring shall bow;

Let lobsters raw with their truncheons roar
"Disperse" to the pugilistic corps -
The pinks of the Prize Ring, in freedom nurs'd
Shall tell them undaunted to do their worst

Shall proclaim to the trap 'tis weak and vain
To seek the brave boxer to restrain
And better 'twould be by far to grab
Those who settle disputes by a mortal stab: -

By Heaven, 'tis sufficient to make us blush
For those who are seeking fair play to crush,
To extinguish courage and skill and game,
And in letters of blood stamp England's shame

Keen in the morning, the glittering snow
Mantles the hills and the vales below,
The landscape around is bleak and bare,
Chill'd by the nipping and frosty air;

The northeast cold over land and sea
Is whistling a sharp, shrill melody;
But the sun is up and the morning bright,
So hasten, brave boys, to the field of fight

This day will decide whether Caunt or Nick
In the shape of conquest shall do the trick -
This day shall to Fancy lads declare
Which hero the Champion's belt shall wear -

Whether Ben, the athletic of giant limb,
Shall yield to young Ward or Nick to him,
And after contention fierce and tough
Which combatant first shall sing "enough"

From slumber rouse, let no time be lost,
Forward for Stockbridge through snow and frost,
Near which, when with creature comfort warmed,
Shall the stakes be pitch'd and the ring be form'd

Strong was the muster upon that day
Of plebeians low and Corinthians gay,
But the beaks for Hants had in anger vow'd
No mill in their county should be allow'd

Looks of despair the Fancy put on,
And determin'd to make a move to Sutton,
And thither hasten'd the fistic ranks,
With policemen hanging upon their flanks;

Then Captain Robbins, with gaze intense,
Cried, "Gentlemen, meaning no offence,
You mustn't attempt, or I'm a liar,
To settle your matters in this here shire"

Now suppose the Fancy, each peril pass'd,
As Crookham Common arriv'd at last,
Prepar'd for superior milling works
Without meddling traps in the shire of Berks:

Suppose the men in position plac'd,
With arms well up and with muscle brac'd,
Each champion seeming resolved to win,
For the love of glory, as well as tin!

But, ah! it is useless to recite
The details of this brief and no-go fight,
What pepper Nick dealt on the giant's mug,
And how Caunt return'd with a Russian hug;

How Nick, though on serious mischief bent,
Dropped down to steer clear of punishment;
And how big Caunt, though in tip-top plight,
Hit his foe on his knees and lost the fight

Yet hurrah for the Ring and the bunch of fives!
Like a giant refresh'd the Ring revives,
It awakens again to vigorous life
To scare the assassin and crush the knife

Then welcome to earth as the flowers in spring
Be the glory renew'd of the Fighting Ring,
And over each British boxer brave
Long may the banner of fair play wave

On the Thursday evening of the ensuing week, on the occasion of the giving up of the stakes, which took place at Young Dutch Sam's, in Vinegar Yard, Drury Lane, Big Ben and his friends were there in force and a motion was put forward for a rematch. This was agreed to on both sides and the articles were settled in the following week, for the men to meet again on the 11th of May, 1841, at Long Marsden.

Chapter 6

CHAMPION OF ENGLAND!

(1841)

At the side of Drury Lane Theatre there was an old tavern known as the Black Lion. It was a celebrated house in the 1840's at which many of the Fancy spent their time and a favourite haunt for the pugilists of the day. It stood in Vinegar Yard, Brydges Street not far from where the once renowned Whistling Oyster shop was situated and it was at the Whistling Oyster where the merry sports of the Black Lion would consume the bivalves[23] and wash them down with the beer of the Black Lion.

It was in the year 1840 that the Whistling Oyster burst into notoriety and gained its curious shop sign. Mr. Pearkes was the proprietor and one morning he discovered an oyster, as it lay fattening on oatmeal in one of the tubs, that was really whistling. Anyhow, it produced some sound very like whistling, beyond all question. It might have been that there was some hole in the shell through which this peculiar bivalve made the noise. Hundreds of people came to listen to the remarkable creature and Mr. Pearkes made quite a little fortune and the trade at the Black Lion also reflected the area's popularity as it also increased enormously. The magazine "Punch" even had jokes about it.

Mr. Pearkes re-christened his shop the "Whistling Oyster," and Vinegar Yard became quite a popular place, with a renown that it had never before acquired. It was one evening about twelve months after the debut of this marvellous oyster to be particular, Thursday night, February 11th, 1841 that some scores of sportsmen passed the Whistling Oyster on their way to the Black Lion. It was a nasty foggy night, so evidently some great attraction must have called them out. The boniface of the Black Lion was at that time Young Dutch Sam, one of the finest middle weight boxers of his time, for he had won a dozen battles and never once suffered defeat. The parlour of the Black Lion was filled with sports quite early in the evening and what with the fog, the tobacco smoke and the steaming grogs[24], it must have been difficult to recognise one's friend on the opposite side of the

---

[23] Aquatic molluscs – e.g. oysters, mussels etc.
[24] Strong drink.

table.

The occasion of this meeting was the presentation of the £200 which was won by Nick Ward in his encounter with Ben Caunt, just nine days previously, the stakes which he had gained on February 2nd, at Cookham Common, when Nick, by his shifty tactics and unmanly behaviour, had provoked Big Ben to deal him a foul blow. It was, of course, quite natural that Caunt and his backers were dissatisfied with the issue of this battle and the Nottingham man had challenged his opponent to try conclusions again in three months' time, but Ward had not given any reply. When, however, the money was paid over at the Black Lion and Nick rose to return thanks for the unexpected windfall, he took the opportunity of informing those present that he expected upon that very evening, at his brother's house in Liverpool, arrangements were being made for him to fight Brassey for £100 a side, but that if the negotiations fell through he was quite ready and willing to meet Caunt again.

At the moment that Nick Ward was upon his legs talking in rather a bouncing manner, there was nobody there to represent Caunt, but shortly afterwards Ben, accompanied by Peter Crawley, entered the room. With them was Ben's principal backer, Mr. Swaine, of the Greyhound, Hatfield, where Ben had trained and where he had been staying since the fight. It appears that Caunt was anything but sober and walking straight up to Nick Ward, he said: "Coom, I mean to feight thee again and lick thee; my brass is ready, a hundred pounds." Now Nick, coward as he was, had good manners and indeed was a gentlemanly, civil young fellow, with a manner in strange contrast to the blustering Caunt, so he politely informed the Nottingham man, as he had already informed the company, that if Brassey did not decide to meet him he should be happy to accommodate Caunt once more.

Ben in an exceedingly coarse manner laughed rudely and snapped his fingers in Nick's face and expressed an opinion that Ward was a cur and a coward. Those who were present say that Nick Ward's pale countenance blushed crimson and to the surprise of everybody, particularly Caunt, he said with no little expression of spirit and determination, "Look here, Mr. Caunt, I spoke to you fair and civilly and you've answered me like a blackguard. I'll let you see whether I'm a cur, a coward or not. Off with your coat and I'll fight you here in the room for love, just to see which is the better man."

Nobody was taken more aback than Ben Caunt at this. He could hardly believe his ears. Then they both peeled off their coats and it looked very much like business then and there and no doubt there would have been a savage set to had not Tom Spring been present. He declared that if they attempted that sort of thing in Sam's house they would lose Sam his licence and the Dutchman, who had been absent when the quarrel took place, came into the room and soon put his veto on the matter. Then Tom Spring insisted upon them shaking hands, which they did reluctantly, advising them to keep their fisticuffs until they again entered the ring. Then it was arranged that they should meet on the following Thursday, February 18th 1841 at the same house and if Nick Ward was found to be free, they were to sign articles and deposit £20 each.

Accordingly, the men with their backers met and both seemed in a very amiable mood and were well attended. Tom Spring, Mr. Swaine and Peter Crawley were there for Caunt and Nick Ward had two friends of his brother Jem, Mr. Munro and Mr. Coleman and a Liverpool friend named Aspinall. The agreeable announcement was made that the match between Ward and Brassey had fallen through and that Nick was therefore at liberty to fight Caunt.

So the coast was clear and the £20 deposit made on each side and the articles drawn up and placed in Mr. Dowling's hands after being duly signed and witnessed.

The document contained the usual clauses:
The said Benjamin Caunt agrees to fight the said Nick Ward a fair stand up fight in a four and twenty foot roped ring, half-minute time, according to the New Rules, for one hundred pounds a side, half way between London and Liverpool. The place to be decided by toss at the last deposit; neither place to exceed twenty miles from the direct line of road, unless mutually agreed upon to the contrary.

The fight to take place on Tuesday May 11th 1841.

The ropes and stakes to be paid for by the men - share and share alike. Neither man to use resin or other powder to his hands during the combat. The parties winning the toss for choice of place were to inform their opponent and backers the name the ground seven days before the fight.

Ben Caunt

The men to be in the ring between twelve and one o'clock, or at an earlier hour if mutually agreed upon, or the money down to be forfeited by the party absent. Two umpires and a referee to be chosen on the ground with the decision of the latter in the event of dispute, to be conclusive. In case of magisterial interference the stakeholder to name the next time and place of meeting, unless a referee shall have been chosen to whom that duty shall be assigned. The fight to come off on the same day if possible; but the money not to be given up till fairly won or lost by a fight.

In pursuance of this agreement £20 a side were deposited there and then at the Black Lion.

A second deposit of £10 a side to be made on Thursday, the 25th of February 1841 at Mr. Swain's The Greyhound at Woodside, Hatfield. A third deposit of £10 a side at The Black Lion, Vinegar Yard, on Thursday the 11th of March. A fourth deposit of £10 a side at Mr Adcock's The Bell at Hatfield on 18th of March. A fifth deposit of £10 a side at Mr Coleman's The Cherry Tree, Kingsland Road on Thursday the 25th of March. A sixth deposit of £10 a side at Jem Ward's The Star in Williamson Square in Liverpool on 1st April. A seventh deposit of £10 a side at the Castle Tavern, Holborn on Thursday the 8th April. An eighth deposit of £10 a side at (unknown) on 15th April. The ninth and last deposit of £10 a side at Young Dutch Sam's, the Black Lion in Vinegar Yard on Thursday the 22nd of April.

Mr Swaine of the Greyhound and Mr. Adcock of the Bell were Ben Caunt's main backers.

The said deposits to be made between the hours of eight and ten o'clock, or the party failing to pay a due deposit to forfeit all the money so far deposited.

The parties, after signing, shook hands with great good humour and joined in drinking the general toast; "May the best man win" Caunt expressed much mortification at the assertion that he said had been made that the cause of his loss of the late fight was attributable to design rather than accident. He protested that he acted from the ungovernable impulse of the moment; irritated by Ward's going down at the moment he was within his reach. He said further, that he would profit by his experience and would be especially careful to avoid a similar "accident". The backers of Ward offered to take six to four on the issue; but odds were refused.

Both men went to their former training quarters - Caunt to Hatfield, Ward to West Derby - and progressed in first-rate style until a fortnight before the fight, when Ben met with a mishap. He was taking one of his long walks, when he accidentally trod on a rolling stone which twisted his ankle with such force that it strained the muscles very severely, so that he was compelled to lay up. Not being able to put his feet to the ground for nearly a week was scarcely the kind of thing for a man training for a fight for the Championship, but Caunt had to grin and bear it. Fortunately, he had excellent surgical advice, so that he was sufficiently recovered to resume his exercise for the last week before the fight.

With the final deposit duly made, Young Dutch Sam, who acted on Nick Ward's behalf, won the toss for choice of ground and named Stratford-upon-Avon for the place of meeting. The selection of Shakespeare's birthplace proved judicious, as the proceedings from first to last passed off without interruption. Another reason for Nick Ward to be keen to fight at Stratford-upon-Avon was because it was there, in July 1831, his brother Jem closed his brilliant career by defeating Simon Byrne at Willycuts, three miles from the town.

So on the Monday afternoon both claimants for the Championship arrived at Stratford-upon-Avon. Tom Spring journeyed to the Warwickshire town with Ben Caunt and they put up at the Red Lion, while Nick Ward, with his brother Jem, made the White Lion his headquarters. Besides these there arrived a couple of brace of other gladiators, who were to do battle in the same ring as the two big 'uns. These were Peter Taylor and Levi Eckersley paired off together and Fred Mason (the Bulldog) and Stephen Puttock, who were expected to give a fine display. So there was an excellent programme, sufficient to draw the sports down in their hundreds.

Indeed, so great was the influx of visitors on the evening before the fights that every hostelry was full to overflowing and sleeping accommodation could not be had for love or money and many had to make their way to Leamington, Warwick and to Coventry with the prospect of a return journey to Stratford in the morning. Reports of the evening regarding the many followers of the foursquare Ring state that the utmost order and regularity prevailed in the town throughout the evening. Hilarity, joviality and good temper prevailed among the partisans of both men, a fact important to record.

The hunting season had not been long over and many sportsmen delayed their departure from the shires so that they might be present at such a field day, for it was rarely that one could witness a fight for the Championship and a couple of first class mills thrown in on the same day.

From Melton, Loughborough, Market Harborough, Rugby and Leamington the hunting men came on their way south. They included such distinguished sportsmen as the Earl of Wilton, Lord Kennedy, Lord Deerhurst, Lord Chetwynd, the veteran Sir Bellingham Graham, Squire Osbaldestor, Captain Horatio Ross, Lord Southampton, Sir William Maxwell, Captain John White and many other well known followers of the chase; whilst from London had come Fulwar Craven, "Ginger" Stubbs, Lord William Lennox, Mr. Richard Tattersall, the Duke of Beaufort, the Marquis of Queensberry, Lord Longford, Lord Wharncliffe, Sir St. Vincent Cotton, Tom Crommelin, the Bishop of Bond Street, Baron Renton Nicholson, Jem Burn and many other notable stars of the Fancy.

The morning of the fight was beautiful and the place was literally besieged. The spot chosen for the battle was Long Marsden, about five miles from Stratford, where a farmer named Pratt, who was an enthusiastic sportsman, offered a large meadow for the purpose of pitching the ring. Tom Oliver and his assistant, Tom Callas, were early on the spot with stakes and tackle. Tom Spring had some days before collected from the swells about £20 for the purpose of engaging a score of pugilists from London and Birmingham to keep order and these special constables were augmented by about a dozen of Mr. Pratt's labourers, who each received half a crown and were provided with stiff ash sticks in case of a disturbance. The choice of venue had been a good one as one side the ground sloped and formed a "rake" which enabled everybody to get a splendid view of the ring.

The people on foot would usually suffer the most on the journey to the scene of the action but on this day they had undoubtedly the best of it. For the pedestrians, by means of short cuts and familiar paths, shortened their pleasant journey, but those who were on four legs, or even worse, on wheels, were compelled to scramble and jolt over roads of the most villainous description, in which the most imminent risks of spills or a break-down were only avoided by care and good luck. In fact, many of those who endured the miseries of both journeys for the two fights between these two fighters declared, that the sixteen miles between the Andover road and Crookham Common, with all its horrors, was surpassed by the shorter journey from Stratford to Long Marsden.

The spot was admirably selected and the ropes and stakes pitched upon a piece of sound, elastic turf that delighted the cognoscenti. The immense multitude, as they arrived, arranged themselves in a most orderly, methodical manner. The day was beautiful, the country around green, fresh and odoriferous with the blossoms of the May. Everything was conducted in a style to ensure general satisfaction.

At half past twelve Ward and Caunt made their appearance amidst a burst of cheering, with Ward escorted by his seconds, Harry Holt, the Cicero of the Ring and Dick Curtis; the Nottingham man by old Ben Butler and Bill Atkinson. Before the men entered the ring Harry Holt, with the new belt, which he exhibited and handed round to the swells in the outer ring to look at, made quite an eloquent speech prepared for the occasion, for Harry was a great orator.

Caunt made his appearance first, with an oddly assorted pair of seconds as ever handled a champion in the Prize Ring. They were old Ben Butler, his uncle, well known in after times in the parlour of the Coach and Horses, a man well stricken in years and a cross-grained old curmudgeon to boot. With him appeared Atkinson, of Nottingham, a 9½ stone man, whose disparity of size with the man he was supposed to pick up excited the risibility of ring-goers. Ben himself, however, seemed particularly well satisfied and remarked laughingly, in a reply to a jocose observation of a bystander, "Never thee mind - I'm not goin' to tumble down; he's big enough for me!" Had the fight which ensued been of the desperate character of Ben's late encounter with Brassey, the ill-assorted pair could about as much have carried Colossus Caunt to his corner as they could have carried the Achilles in Hyde Park. Nick had with him, as on the former occasion, Harry Holt and Dick Curtis, certainly the two ablest counsellors on the Midland, Northern, or any other Circuit.

Tom Spring, who was in friendly attendance upon Caunt, addressed an emphatic warning to the Big 'Un to keep his temper, cautioning him not to play into the hands of his opponent by allowing himself to be irritated by his shifty dodges. Caunt listened with a grim, self-satisfied smile and nodded his head, as much as to say he was not going to be caught this time.

Each man, in reply to a question, declared he "never felt better in his life," and his looks justified the assertion. Caunt was a little "finer drawn" than at their previous meeting and weighed, when stripped, exactly 14st. 6lb. He never went to scale so light before - indeed, it was not an excessive weight for a big-boned man measuring 6 feet 2½ inches. Ward looked to be a trifle too fleshy. He weighed 13st. 6lb., 10lb. more than when he fought in February.

Some time previously a subscription had been raised to produce a Champion's belt, to be given to the victor on this occasion and to be hereafter transferable, should he retire from the Prize Ring or be beaten by a more successful candidate for fistic honours. This belt, under the superintendence of a committee, was completed and now for the first time was held forth as an additional incitement to bravery and good conduct. Previous to the commencement of the battle, Cicero Holt, the well-known orator of the Prize Ring and second of Nick Ward, approached the scratch and silence being called, held up the belt, pronouncing that in addition to the stakes this trophy had been prepared by a number of liberal gentlemen, as a spur to the honest and manly feeling which it was desirable should ever pervade the minds of men who sought distinction in the Prize Ring. "Honour and fair play," it was their opinion, should be the motto of English boxers and it would be their proud gratification to see this belt girded round the loins of him, whoever he might be, who entitled himself in spirit and principle to the terms of that motto. They were influenced by neither favour nor affection, nor by prejudice of any kind; all they desired was that the best man might win, wear this trophy and retain it so long as he was enabled to maintain the high and distinguished title of Champion of England. On resigning, or being stripped of the laurels of Championship, it would then be his duty to transfer his proud badge to his more fortunate successor and thus a prize would be established which it would ever be the pride of gallant Englishmen to possess and its brightness, he trusted, would never be tarnished by an act of dishonour. It was to be finally presented, he said, when complete, at a dinner to be given at Jem Burn's where the subscription originated, on Monday, the 31st instant.

The belt was then exhibited to the gaze of the curious; it was composed of purple velvet and lined with leather; in the centre were a pair of clasped hands surrounded by a wreath of the Rose, the Thistle and the Shamrock, entwined in embossed silver; on each side of this were three shields of bright silver, at the time without inscription, but on these were to be engraved the names of all the Champions of England which the records of the Fancy preserve, to conclude with the name of the conqueror on the present occasion. The clasps in front were formed of two hands encased in sparring gloves. Its inspection afforded general pleasure and the oration of "Cicero" was received with loud cheers. Caunt, on taking it in his hand, significantly said to Nick Ward, "This is mine, Nick," to which Ward replied, "I hope the best man may win it and wear it."

These preliminaries, so novel in the Prize Ring, having been concluded, the colours of the men were entwined on the stake and umpires and a referee having been chosen, no time was lost in preparing for action. At twenty minutes to one all was ready and the champions toed the scratch. The referee called "Time," and the two men having once more shaken hands, they put up their fists and commenced to fight for the handsome trophy and the Championship of England.

THE FIGHT

Round 1:
The men faced each other with an expression of good humour on their countenances that could hardly be expected by those who knew how they had expressed themselves at former meetings. Caunt's rough lineaments bore a grin of satisfaction that seemed to say he had his wishes gratified. Ward, though he also smiled, it was a vanishing smile and he looked eagerly and anxiously at his antagonist. Ward's attitude was scientific and well guarded, his left ready for a lightening-shot; as he poised himself on his left toe, with his right somewhat across, to parry the possible counter hit. Caunt stood erect, as if to make the most of his towering height, but a trifle backward. Ward moved about a little, as if measuring his distance and then let go his left. It was not a determined hit and did not get home. Caunt dashed out his left in return, but Nick stopped it prettily. However, as he meant it for a counter, his friends were pleased at his quickness and cheered the attempt, especially as he almost instantly followed it with a lunge from the right, which just reached Ward's neck. The big one now bored in for a close, meaning mischief. Ward bobbed his head aside, delivered a slight job and was down on his knees. It was clear that he meant to fight in the evasive style of their former encounter, but it was also clear from Caunt's coolness that he was likely to have more trouble over this day's business.

Round 2:
The men faced each other as before, no harm as yet having been done on either side. Caunt now began manoeuvring in rather an ungainly manner; but as some of his movements suggested a plunge in, Nick was resolved to be first and let go his left on Caunt's mouth, who heeded not the blow, but dashed out left and right. The blows were wild, but his right reached Ward's cheek; Caunt was pulling himself together for heavy punching, when once more Ward slipped his foot and was on both knees. Caunt threw up both hands and gave a sort of guttural "Hur!, hur!" as he looked at the cunning face of his opponent, then walked to his own corner. The Big 'Un's friends were delighted at this proof of caution and cheered lustily.

Round 3:
Ward came up with a keen and anxious look at his opponent. Ben nodded and flourished his long arms like the sails of a windmill. He seemed ready to let Ward lead off and then take his chance of going in for the return. Ward drew back at arm's length and Caunt hit short more than once, but Nick did not get near enough for an effective return. Caunt, with a grim smile, almost rolled in, sending out left and right as he came. His right just reached Ward's head, who hit up sharply and then slipped down, as though from his own blow. It was a very questionable get-down, but there was no appeal.

Round 4:
Nick seemed to feel that he was by no means taking the lead and he was told that unless he hit and kept Caunt employed in defending himself, he would bore in on him continually. The advice was doubtless sound, but it wanted more courage than Nick possessed to put it into practice. Nick hit out with his left, but not near enough and Caunt stopped him, amid some cheering; Caunt paused, as if expecting Ward to come closer, but he did not, so he let fly and in a sort of ding-dong rally gave Ward a tidy smack on the nose; Nick jobbed him heavily three or four times, then dropped so close to Caunt that they both rolled over, the Big 'Un falling heavily on Nick. On rising, blood was seen oozing from Ward's nose and the first event was awarded to Caunt, amidst the cheers of his friends and the astonishment of Ward's backers.

Round 5:
The faces of both men were flushed from the blows received and Caunt, who was anxious to be at work, went in at once, left and right, again

catching Ward upon the nose and increasing the appearance of claret. Ward made no return, he was too anxious to get away and on Caunt grappling him, he got quickly down, Caunt stumbling forward and falling over him.

Round 6:
The rounds were too short and hurried to admit of much in the way of description. Caunt, still eager to be at work, tried his left, but was stopped. Counter-hits with the left followed, but though Nick was a fine counter hitter, he never exhibited any great relish for that mode of fighting - the most telling in its effects and most exciting to witness of all practised in the Prize Ring. Caunt lashed out with his left and as Nick cleverly avoided the smash they rushed to in-fighting. Nick, however, pursued his plan of getting down, but Caunt came heavily upon him. Although up to the present time Caunt had not done much execution, yet he was certainly getting the best of the fight and he maintained his improvement in his style of hitting, substituting straight hits from the shoulder for the over handed chops which had formerly marked his attempts.

Round 7:
Ward tried to regain the lead - if he had ever had it - and let fly with his left, but he had not sufficient courage to go close to his man and once again the blow fell short. He stopped Caunt's attempt at a return with his left, which came pretty heavy and quickly, and on the latter's rushing in for close work Nick dropped on his knees. There was no blow struck in this round and Caunt, about to deliver, wisely restrained his hand and with his deep, short laugh, shook his finger menacingly at Ward as he knelt and walked away.

Round 8:
Up to this period no material damage had been done on either side, few of the hits having more than a skin deep effect. Ward still preserved his elegant attitude and tried his left, but did not get home and Caunt hit short at the body with his right. Nick now steadied himself for mischief and, after a short pause, threw his left with the quickness of lightening and caught Caunt over the right eyebrow, on which it left a gaping wound, from which a copious crimson stream flowed over the undamaged optic and down his cheek. Caunt hit out wildly, left and right; Ward, in retreating, fell on his knees and Caunt tumbled over him.

Round 9:
Atkinson was seen to be busily engaged in stopping the flow of claret from Caunt's eyebrow when "Time" was called. At the sound Caunt jumped up vigorously and continued the contest with a figurehead anything but improved by the crimson stain, which marked its right side. Nick smiled at his handiwork, waited for his man and as Caunt came plunging in, met him with a heavy hit from the left on the cheek, opening an ancient wound originally inflicted by Brassey and starting a fresh tap of claret. Caunt was stung by the hits and dashed in left and right; but Ward adhered to his dropping tactics and again fell on his knees, amidst strong expressions of disapprobation.

Round 10:
Ward again tried his left, but was unsuccessful; Caunt came in and after a couple of slight exchanges, left and right, Nick got down.

Round 11:
Caunt came up nothing daunted, stopped an attempt with Ward's left and made a terrific rush, which if as clumsy as the elephant's was almost as irresistible. Nick retreated, stopping left and right, till he fell under the ropes, amidst cries of dissatisfaction, Caunt dropping on him.

Round 12:
Ward stopped Caunt's left and right and almost immediately dropped on his knees and while in that position instantly hit up left and right, delivering both blows heavily; that from his right, on Caunt's ear, from whence blood was drawn, was evidently a stinger. Spring, who witnessed this, exclaimed against so cowardly a practice and observed that the blows of Ward were obviously foul, in as much as Ward had no more right to hit when down on his knees than Caunt had a right to strike him in that position. The umpires, however, did not interfere and the referee cautioned Ward to be more circumspect in his conduct.

Round 13:
Caunt, lively as a young buffalo, rushed to the scratch the moment "Time" was called and immediately made play. Nick, as usual, retreated when Caunt endeavoured to close and Nick in his cowardly way dropped on both knees. Caunt's right hand was up and he was unable to restrain the falling blow, but it fell lightly and although "down" no claim was made. (Spring and Atkinson both cautioned Caunt to be more careful, for, however

unintentional, if he struck his opponent when down the consequences might be serious.)

Round 14:
Caunt led off and caught Nick on the side of the head with his left and repeated the dose on the opposite side with his right. Nick popped in a touch with his left on Caunt's nasal promontory - Caunt missed a terrific hit with his right and Nick went on his knees to avoid punishment.

Round 15:
Caunt, who was now evidently provoked by the cowardly game of Ward in getting down in every round, the moment he came to the scratch rushed to him and endeavoured to get him within his grasp in such a way as to be enabled to fall with him. Unluckily, however, instead of catching him round the body he caught him round the neck and, in this manner, lifting him off the ground, for a short time held him suspended. He then let him go, but did not succeed in giving him the scrunch he contemplated. Instead of this, he hit the back of his own head against the stakes and incurred an ugly concussion.

Round 16:
Caunt came up full of life and frolic and was first at the scratch. Nick made play with his left, but Caunt stopped and got away. Caunt hit short with his right and after a short pause right-hand hits were exchanged - Nick at the head, Caunt at the body. Caunt immediately closed and caught Nick's pimple under his arm, but Nick slipped down and looked up as if expecting to be hit.

Round 17:
Trifling exchanges, when Nick again provokingly slipped on his knees.

Round 18:
Caunt led off, planted his left slightly and Nick went down on his knees. Caunt looked at him derisively and laughed, exclaiming, "It won't do today, Nick"

Round 19:
Caunt, still fresh as a four-year-old was first to the scratch, Nick evidently fearful of approaching too near. Caunt made a feint, with his left and then delivered a tremendous round right-handed blow on the base of Ward's

ribs; the blow was too high, or it might have told fearfully. Nick let go his left and Caunt jumped back, but again coming to the charge Ward retreated. Caunt following him up again seized him with a Herculean grip round the neck, lifted him clean off the ground and then fell squash upon him.

Round 20:
Some tolerably good exchanges, in which Nick hit straightest, but then immediately, went down with Caunt pointing at him with contempt.

Round 21:
Nick tried his left and right, but missed, his timidity evidently preventing his getting sufficiently near to his man. Caunt again seized him, lifted him up and fell upon him, but lightly.

Round 22:
Caunt hit a short at the body with his right and tried his left, which was stopped. Counter-hits with the right, ditto with the left, when Nick went down.

Round 23:
Ward planted his left heavily on Caunt's mug and opened his previous wounds; this he followed with a touch from his right on the ear. Caunt rushed wildly to the charge, but Nick, as usual, tumbled, this time rolling over away from Caunt.

Round 24:
Caunt rushed forward and delivered his left and right on Ward's nob, the first on his nose, the second on the side of his head; Ward's nose again trickled with the purple fluid. Nick went down on his knees, amidst shouts of disapprobation.

Round 25:
Caunt delivered his left on the head and right on the body, with stinging effect and Nick went down.

Round 26:
Nick again had it on his nose from the left and dropped on his knees. Caunt, who had his right up with intent to deliver, withheld the blow and walked away.

Round 27:
Nick slow in approaching the scratch and Caunt impatient to be at him. Holt cautioned Caunt not to cross the scratch till his man reached it. Caunt let fly with his right and again caught Nick heavily on the body, following this up with a smart touch from his left on the mazzard[25]. Nick again went down on one knee and, while in that position, struck Caunt with his left. Caunt stooped, nodded and laughed at him. As he looked up in his face. Nick also nodded and laughed. "We'll have a fair fight today, Nick," said Caunt.

Round 28:
Good counter-hits with the left, when Caunt once more grasped Ward and held him up; but Ward slipped from his arms and got down.

Round 29:
Ward slow, when Caunt planted two right handed hits on his jaw and neck. Ward slipped down on one knee, but Caunt refrained from striking him, although entitled to do so by the rules of the Prize Ring.

Round 30:
Caunt lost no time in rushing to his man and planted his right heavily on the side of his head. Ward hit widely left and right and went down on his face.

Round 31:
Ward evidently began to lose all confidence and fought extremely shy. Caunt rushed in, caught Ward's head under his arm and although he might have hit him with great severity, he restrained himself and let him fall.

Round 32:
Ward came up evidently counter to his own inclinations, being urged forward by his seconds. Caunt caught him left and right and he fell to avoid further punishment.

Round 33:
Caunt gave a lunging slap with his right on Ward's pimple, when Ward dropped on both knees and popped his head between Caunt's knees. He seemed disposed to poke in anywhere out of danger's way and any odds

---

[25] The head

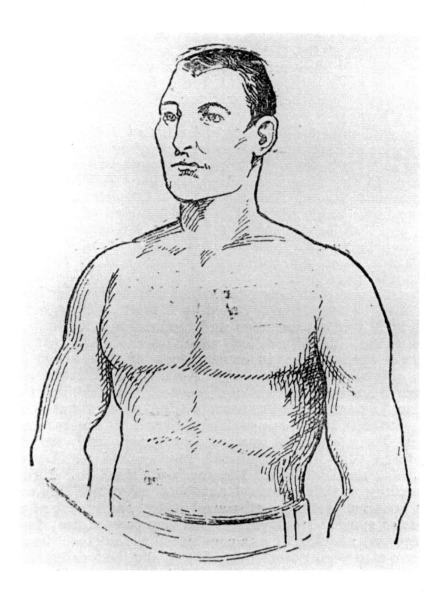

Nick Ward – Who Ben fought twice for the championship

were offered on Caunt.

Round 34:
Caunt rushed in to mill, but Ward had obviously made up his mind to be satisfied and down he went without a blow and there were loud cries of "Take him away, take the cur out of the ring."

Round 35:
Ward's second and bottle holder Harry Holt and Curtis persuaded him to go up for one more. Then Ben went for him with right and left in the face and down Nick dropped for the last time. His brother Jem ducked under the ropes and implored him to fight one plucky round for the credit of the family, but Nick had had enough and lay groaning, declaring that Caunt had broken his ribs. This excuse didn't impose upon brother Jem. He turned away disdainfully and holding up his hand, said, " You've won, Ben!"

Caunt was thus proclaimed the conqueror and "THE CHAMPION OF ENGLAND," amidst wild cheering from his supporters.

Such was Caunt's exhilaration on winning and becoming champion that on quitting the ring, he disdained to do so in the usual way and leaped clear over the top rope, a height of four feet six.

While Caunt was being cheered, there were only expressions of contempt towards Ward, so much so that Holt omitted the usual collection for the losing man. Holt shook a hat containing only a few halfpenny pieces he had himself dropped into it and then put them in his pocket with a laugh.

Ward had the supposed fracture in his ribs examined, but nothing could be discovered beyond severe contusions. It will be recollected that Brassey closed his labours with Caunt upon similar grounds, though perhaps with better reason. Nick was immediately conveyed to his omnibus, where he became prostrate in mind and body, exciting but little sympathy in the breasts of the general body of spectators. The fight lasted forty-seven minutes. The ceremony of girding Caunt with the Champion's belt then took place and it was put round his loins, with a hearty wish from those who witnessed his unflinching courage from first to last, as well as his manly forbearance amidst cowardly provocation, that he might long retain it. He afterwards went to Ward's carriage and offered him all the consolations of which he was susceptible, hoping that they might hereafter be the best of friends, a feeling that Jem Ward, who evidently blushed for the pusillanimity of his brother, good-naturedly reciprocated. Caunt, he said, had proved himself the better man and should always be an acceptable guest at his house.

Caunt then ran part of the way home by running a pretty fast race against a Corinthian[26] across a piece of ploughed land for the prize of a bottle of wine, which he duly won.

In summary, the report of this fight tells its own tale. Nick Ward's conduct completely confirmed the suspicions of his chicken-hearted pretensions. He wanted that one requisite of all others indispensable to a pugilist – courage. Although his science was unquestionable, it can only be displayed to advantage in the sparring school. As he said himself after his fight with Sutton, he "was not cut out for a fighting man;" and the best advice any man could give him would be to retire altogether from the Prize Ring. Caunt, who from the first booked victory as certain, sustained his character for bravery and left off as fresh as when he commenced, although somewhat damaged in the frontispiece. His right eyebrow and cheek were much swollen and the back of his head displayed a prominent bump of combativeness from the fall against the stakes. His hands were little damaged, but the knuckle of his right hand showed that it had come in ugly contact with Nick's pimple or ribs. He was much improved in his style of fighting since his former exhibitions in the Prize Ring; instead of hitting over the guard, as was his former practice, he hit straight from the shoulder and having learned to lead off with his left, was enabled the more effectively to bring the heavy weight of his right into useful play. He still, however, hit round with his right and the most severe blows which Ward received during the contest were those which were planted on the ribs and side of the head with this hand. These blows, with the heavy falls, to which was added the weight of his antagonist, no doubt tended to extinguish the little courage he might have possessed. Caunt was carefully seconded by his aged uncle and Atkinson and although, had it been necessary to carry him to his corner, they might not have been able to afford him the requisite assistance As that necessity did not arise no fault was to be found. Throughout the battle excellent order was maintained and there were none of those irregularities observable on the former occasion. Jem Ward and his friends conducted themselves with great propriety and submitted to

---

[26] An amateur sportsman

defeat as well as to the loss of their money with as good a grace as could well have been expected. To the amateurs and patrons of British boxing the conduct of Nick Ward was most displeasing and they one and all declared that they had never seen a man whose pretensions to the Championship had been more disgracefully exposed. Caunt came to town the same night, accompanied by Tom Spring and on reaching the Castle was received with universal congratulations.

This fight was Nick's "Waterloo," and his last appearance on any field. He became a publican, first in Liverpool and then in London and on the 17th of February, 1850, departed this life, at the King's Head, Compton Street, Soho, the victim of a pulmonary attack.

On the Monday evening of 7th of June 1841, a month after Ben had fought and beaten Ward, an express arrived at Hucknall, stating that Benjamin Caunt was on his way to his native village. This sent general excitement through the inhabitants, it being the first view they had had of him since his recent victory over Ward to become the Champion of England. A large door was laid across a cart, drawn by a number of young men, in the centre of which was affixed a large armchair and a bean rod graced with a large handkerchief as a substitute for a flag. Musicians, with brass and other instruments and also a drum, set out with the expedition to meet the 'conquering hero' and when they met him he mounted the chair and was borne along in triumph, preceded by a number of men with green oak boughs. But reverses are common to all men and when the procession reached the bottom of the town the chair broke and down came the Champion of England to his mother earth. The conqueror was not much hurt, but would not again ascend ambition's height and preferred walking to his quarters at the Coach and Six.

Caunt headed the parade dressed in a yellow muffler and plum coloured waistcoat with the championship belt around his waist. Ben marched into Hucknall to a tremendous reception by the townsfolk. Once inside the Old Coach and Six Inn with the children of the town gathered outside to see him, Ben, a bit of a practical joker, heated some farthings on a shovel then hurled them through the window, laughing uproariously as the children tried to pick them up. Dancing and celebrating continued until the following morning.

Chapter 7

THE CHAMPION VISITS AMERICA

(1841-1843)

Caunt decided to follow the fashion of other notable public performers, to make a trans Atlantic trip, to show the New World a specimen of an Old World champion and to add another 'big thing' to the country of big things. As it was to turn out, America sustained her eminence by sending us an even bigger 'champion' than Big Ben himself.

So in September 1841 Ben sailed to America with the event announced in the English press on Friday 10th of September as follows: 'Ben Caunt, Champion of England, sailed from Liverpool for New York on Thursday, taking with him the Champion's belt, for which he says, any Yankee may become a candidate'.

In the American newspaper New York Spirit of the Times of Saturday 13th of November was the following paragraph:

'Caunt, the Champion of England, arrived on Monday week last in the packet ship Europe, bringing with him the Champion's belt. He has appeared several times at the Bowery Theatre, in 'Life in London,' being introduced in the scene opening with Tom Cribb's sparring-room. He is an immensely powerful man, two or three inches above six feet in height and well proportioned. Caunt's reputation at home is that of a liberal, manly fellow; prodigious strength and thorough game have won him more battles than his science, though he is no chicken.'

The following challenge also appeared in some of the American daily papers:

'Challenge - To Caunt, the Champion of England, - Sir, I will fight you for 500 dollars, three months from this date, the forfeit money to be put up at any time and place you may name. You can find me at 546, Grand Street. - Yours, JAMES JEROLOMON.'"

This challenge was of course, mere 'buncombe' and appears to have been an attempt to publicise and raise the profile of the tour.

Caunt published the following:
I declare my intention of not fighting in America, but if anything can tempt me to change my intention, it will be the following circumstances:-

When at Philadelphia I intended taking a Southern tour, but an unexpected circumstance brought me back to New York. There appeared a challenge in the papers of New York from the Michigan Giant to me; my friends at New York went to try to make a match with him; they offered to back me for ten thousand dollars a side and sent for me to return as soon as possible. There is no match made yet, but it is likely there will be soon. I am quite prepared to fight him - he is the only man who could draw me from my first determination. This Giant is seven feet three inches high, proportionally stout and very active; he can turn twenty-five somersaults in succession, can hold a large man out at arm's length, he weighs 333lb and has nothing but muscle on his bones. I have all reasons to believe a match will be made. I expect to be in England in a short time if the above match is not made, when I shall be ready to accommodate Bendigo. You will oblige me by inserting some or the whole of the above in your valuable columns.
I remain, Yours, &c.,
BENJAMIN CAUNT
New York,
December 20th, 1841.

Interesting to note that in a different (New York) newspaper the "Michigan Giant" becomes the "New York Baby," without any mention of fistic collision between the so-called 'champions.'

According to an ex justice of police the amateurs of the Ring have been in a state of excitement and anticipation ever since the arrival of the English Champion, Caunt. He has just concluded a successful engagement at one of the Philadelphia theatres, after having appeared several nights here at the Bowery, in 'Life in London.' Caunt has put on the gloves for a friendly set-to with most of our amateurs at Hudson's 'Sparring Rooms and Pistol Gallery,' on the corner of Broadway and Chambers Street; he hits hard and is as active as a 'bottled imp.'

It turned out that 'The American Giant' was Charles Freeman who was born in Michigan and was about six feet, six inches tall and weighed over two hundred and fifty pounds. He had never entered the regular Prize Ring, yet in 1841 he challenged the English champion, Benjamin Caunt, who was

S.S. Europe in which Ben sailed to America

touring in Philadelphia, to a sparring match. Before long the two were exhibiting together in a number of American cities.

Although the names and stories of his height and weight continued to vary tremendously, Freeman was indeed a fine specimen. He had immense muscular developments and was well put together, 'with arms and legs strong enough for the working-beam or piston-rod of a Mississippi steamboat'. He could lift fifteen hundredweight and could throw an astounding number of somersaults in succession and run and jump like a deer.

Caunt had just returned from a visit through the British Provinces and at Halifax, he received a challenge, which was accepted, but upon seeing the 'New York Baby,' waived the honour of meeting him, except with the muffles on.

Freeman knew almost nothing about professional boxing. After gazing upon his huge frame and witnessing his feats of great strength and agility, Caunt decided that did not matter. He envisioned great things for Freeman in the Prize Ring and persuaded the young man to return with him to London.

Before leaving, Caunt tipped off the New York press. The writers, of course, pounced on the story. They built Freeman up, giving him a fictitious record, while the editors caught their readers' attention with headlines proclaiming that the huge American was crossing the Atlantic to lay claim to the 'Championship of the World.'

In actual fact Caunt saw the financial possibilities of touring Britain as The Champion of England sparring with 'The Champion of The World'.

After a profitable and pleasant tour, in which, as he declared on his return, he met nothing but hospitality and civility from our American cousins, Ben returned to England in March 1842, accompanied by Charles Freeman. Freeman was dubbed, for circus and theatre purposes, "Champion of the World;" and truly, if bulk and height were the prime requisites of a boxer, then Charles Freeman certainly looked a world champion.

The English sporting crowd was fascinated with Freeman's size and strength and many "sparring tours" were carried out by Ben and his giant partner, including appearances at provincial theatres etc. Indeed the first few nights of the tour were at the Queens Theatre in Liverpool and there was not a seat to be had on any of the evenings.

The visit to America and the subsequent tours with Freeman of the theatres in England proved to be financially very beneficial to Caunt and in July 1842 he took over the Coach and Horses Inn in St. Martin's Lane, London. The Coach and Horses soon had the reputation as one of the major sporting houses in London where fights were arranged, deposits paid and the Fancy would spend their time.

During this period there was always an undercurrent of pugilistic challenges and correspondence kept up in the sporting papers. These included the Tipton Slasher (William Perry) posting a challenge to the American Giant while Bendigo offered terms to Ben.

Meanwhile, during 1842 Bendigo, ignoring the advice of his doctors, made his way to London and putting in an appearance at a 'soiree' at Jem Burn's, solicited the honour of a glove-bout with Peter Crawley. Bendy's resuscitation was hailed with delight and as he declared his readiness to renew a broken-off match with Tass Parker, a spirited patron of the Prize Ring declared that money should be no obstacle. On the Thursday week ensuing, Tass also being in town with his friend for the Derby week, all parties met at Johnny Broome's and articles were penned and duly signed. By these it was agreed that the men should meet on Wednesday, the 24th of August, within twenty miles of Wolverton, in the direction of Nottingham, for a stake of £200 a side. Parker having beaten Harry Preston, the game Tom Britton, of Liverpool and the powerful John Leechman (Brassey, of Bradford), was now at the pinnacle of his fame. His friends too were most confident, as Bendigo's lameness was but too painfully apparent. Tass offered to deposit the value of Bendigo's belt, to be the prize of the victor." The match went on until June 28th, when, £140 being down, it was announced at the fifth deposit that the bold Bendigo was in custody on a warrant issued by his brother (a respectable tradesman in Nottingham), who was averse to his milling pursuits. The rumour was too true. Bendy was brought before their worships, charged with intending a breach of the peace with one Hazard Parker and held to bail to keep the peace towards all Her Majesty's subjects for twelve months, himself in £100 and two sureties of £100 each.

The cup which Ben was wont to exhibit to visitors to St Martin's Lane, as the 'Champion of England's Cup,' was a handsome piece of plate, subscribed for by a number of Ben's admirers and friends in a number of places including Newcastle, Gateshead and Nottingham. It was presented to him at a spread at Izzy Lazarus's Cross Keys Gateshead on the date given in the inscription which was as follows: "Presented to Benjamin Caunt, Champion of England, by his Newcastle friends as a token of respect for his abilities as a pugilist and his conduct as a man, July 6th, 1842."

Johnny Broome called a meeting at his house - The Rising Sun in Air Street Piccadilly - of interested parties as he decided it was time to put Freeman's claims of being 'Champion of the World' to the test.

Tom Spring clarified the situation by saying that Freeman had not come to this country with any intentions to fight, as his pursuits were quite different. Since his arrival in England, Freeman had challenged no one but acknowledged that the advertising placards of his appearances on tour with Caunt did contain a challenge to 'any and every man'. Freeman was an easy going and very likeable man but he had promised he would not avoid a challenge if it came his way.

So as the summer of 1842 waned, Caunt finally agreed a regular ring fight for Freeman against the veteran pugilist William Perry, the "Tipton Slasher," for £100 a side.

After accepting a challenge made by Johnny Broome on behalf of Perry the two men went into serious training. Freeman's regime included walking twenty to thirty miles a day, which, by reducing his excess weight, only served to make his Herculean figure the more imposing. Its symmetry, despite its enormous size, was much admired.

The nationalistic implications of the battle were lost on neither side. A correspondent for the Spirit of the Times reminded Freeman of his patriotic obligations: "Recollect that it is to vindicate her [America's] claims to, at least an equal standing in the sporting world with her great mother, that you have left your own fireside; recollect that every time you strike a blow, every time you take a position, it is to the credit or dishonour of your native land. Let this move your arm and let every blow be emphatically the blow of a Freeman for free-men!" The English sporting press saw the pending struggle in equally nationalistic terms.

Charles Freeman

Unfortunately, the fight failed to live up to the lofty expectations. Arrangements were so poorly made that the two men did not come to the scratch to commence fighting until just after four o'clock. This was far too late on an afternoon in December when the light fails early. Freeman's awkwardness, inexperience and disinclination to fight aggressively, Perry's constant falling without receiving a blow to compensate for his lack of scientific skills, produced an uninspired bout. Ringside thugs exacting tribute from the Fancy did not help matters. So after seventy rounds in one hour and twenty-four minutes of a poor fight, the men were told to leave the ring in the darkness, as the referee would no longer allow them to continue.

The fight was re-arranged for six days later on December 20th and after thirty-seven sloppy rounds in thirty-nine minutes the referee finally disqualified Perry for falling without a blow, giving Freeman the victory.

From the start, it had been an odd contest in pugilistic terms, an exercise for the curious as to how a fighter could tackle an opponent over a foot taller and with commensurate advantages in reach and weight. The Slasher's answer was to dash in and out quickly, to dodge, to try and avoid Freeman's bear-like hugs and shattering throws and to go down on his knees at the first

William Perry – The Tipton Slasher

opportunity, blow or no blow. He did this with such regularity and readiness that the 108 rounds of the whole fight took less than two hours. There could be all manner of excuses for The Slasher's mode of fighting - the grass was slippery, there was no other way to tackle such a giant and (by his own account) the recoil from his own punches on that massive frame caused him to lose his balance! None of the excuses would serve however, once the two umpires at last applied to the referee for a verdict. He immediately pronounced The Slasher's latest fall to be unjustified and foul and the fight was over.

The Slasher had seemed unable to fend off Freeman's blows, while his own attacks were of the wildest, relying for the most part on a swinging right hand. Freeman, by contrast, was a revelation. He had quickly picked up some of the rudiments of orthodox boxing and but for the poor timing of his blows would soon have had his opponent floored.

There was the same contrast in the behaviour of the two men at the handing over of the stakes at Spring's inn, the Castle. Freeman accepted his money with an impressive speech that was both fluent and modest, while The Slasher's response to the few pounds raised by a collection for him was confined to rubbing the side of his nose and a couple of grunts!

The American ring community, though still small, had anticipated a good fight; as the Spirit of the Times put it, "a great degree of excitement pervades our sporting circles as to the result." Shortly after these words were written, however, Tom McCoy's[27] body was interred in Potter's Field. As a result, Charles Freeman's exploits received little coverage in American newspapers and prize-fighting in America virtually ceased.

After his only fight 'in anger' Freeman realised that prize-fighting was not for him and he gave up boxing for the stage. In early 1843, he appeared at the Olympia Theatre in The Son of the Desert and Demon Changeling, a piece written expressly for him. He also did a stint with the circus. "His great circus performance," according to a Hunterian Museum report, "was to ride two horses at a time, galloping around the arena, with his arms above his head balancing a man." Perhaps to make ends meet, he later became a barman at the Lion and Ball tavern in Red Lion Street, Holborn.

---

[27] Irishman Tom McCoy became the first Prize Ring fatality in America during a fight with Englishman Christopher Lilly in Hastings a few miles from New York.

Ben Caunt - with the Cup presented to him by his admirers

The giant barman excited the Lion and Ball's regular crowd and attracted many new patrons, who got to see him for only the price of a whiskey. Either Freeman or one of his promoters penned the following poetic invitation to the British public to visit him:

> You need not unto Hyde Park go,
> For without imposition,
> Smith's Bar Man is and no mistake,
> The true Great Exhibition.
>
> The proudest noble in the land,
> Despite caprice and whim,
> Though looking down on all the world,
> Must fain look up to him.
>
> His rest can never be disturbed
> By chanticleer in song,
> For though he early goes to bed,
> He sleeps so very long.
>
> Though you may boast a many friends,
> Look in and stand a pot;
> You'll make a new acquaintanceship,
> The longest you have got.
>
> Then come and see the Giant Youth,
> Give Edward Smith a call,
> Remember in Red Lion-street,
> The Lion and the Ball.

Sadly Charles Freeman never returned to America and died of tuberculosis on October 18th 1845 at Winchester Hospital – less than three years after his fight with Perry.

Chapter 8

BENDIGO TAKES THE TITLE

(1844-1850)

Bendigo's accident, which occurred in March 1840 had put him out of boxing for some considerable time as well as costing him a forfeit of £75 to Tass Parker for failing to fight, and it was not until the latter part of 1843 that he was sufficiently recovered to feel justified in disputing the claim of Caunt to be the Champion of England.

By the early part of 1844 Bendigo was now very anxious to meet Caunt and the Nottingham man published the following verses in Bell's Life:

> " May I never again take a sip of ' blue ruin,'
> If I love to see fair English fighting take wing -
> 'Tis time for the 'Big 'Un' to be up and doing,
> For bantam cocks only show now in the Ring
>
> Then again for the laurel crown let us be tugging,
> May fair play be always our motto and plan -
> But Caunt I denounce and his system of hugging -
> practice more fit for a bear than a man."

And the following response from Caunt:

A WORD FROM THE CHAMPION.
To the Editor of Bell's Life in London.
Sir, - Seeing a challenge from Bendigo this week, I shall be happy to meet him on his own terms, £200 a side (in which I heartily hope he will not disappoint me). I will meet him at my own house, on Tuesday evening next, to stake not less than £20 as a first deposit. Should this challenge not be accepted, I will fight Bendigo, Tass Parker and the Tipton Slasher, once each within six months, for £200 a side and shall be prepared to deposit £60 - viz., £20 each match - as the first deposit, any time at my house, or at Tom Spring's, the Castle Tavern, Holborn. Should this not be 'a go' within four months, I shall beg most respectfully to decline the Prize Ring altogether.
Ben Caunt.
January 21st, 1844.

On April 17th 1845 at a sporting dinner at Owen Swift's, at which, besides a full muster of Corinthians, Tom Spring, Peter Crawley, Jem Burn, Frank Redmond, Tom Oliver, Dan Dismore, Bill Jones and many of the professionals were present, the matter of the Championship was formally discussed and with the consent of Caunt, Bendigo was matched to fight him on September 9th for £200, Caunt's subscription belt and the Championship.

At the final deposit, on August 26th, at Tom Spring's, the Castle Tavern, Holborn, it was officially announced that both men were in splendid condition. Bendigo had trained at Crosby, near Liverpool, under the care of Jem Ward and Caunt near Hatfield, in Hertfordshire, where he was looked after by his uncle, Ben Butler and by Jem Turner, the D'Orsay of the Prize Ring, besides being constantly visited by his great friend and patron, the gallant Tom Spring. Caunt, who was now thirty-three years of age, had scaled over 17st. when he went into training, but on the day of the fight was reduced to a pound under 14st., the lightest weight he ever reached in any of his fights. Bendigo, who was three years older, weighed 12st. 1lb. and was also in the pink of condition.

When articles were originally signed, on April 17th, it was arranged that the fight should take place half-way between London and Nottingham, but at the final supper this was altered by mutual consent to Newport Pagnell, in Bucks.

On Monday September 8th, the day before the battle was to come off, so great was the interest centred in the affair, hundreds of people journeyed to Wolverton, in the neighbourhood of which the fight was supposed to come off. The weather was fearfully hot and every tavern and lodging that could be had was occupied. Bendigo, accompanied by Jem Ward and Merryman, arrived on the eve of the battle and put up at Tom Westley's house, the Swan.

Jem Ward immediately sought a convenient spot to form the arena and selected the banks of the river Ouse, near where the poet Cowper once resided, some four miles from the town. The excitement was intense in Wolverton, for amongst the latest arrivals was the High Constable, who had instructions to arrest the principals, but Bendigo had timely warning and was smuggled from the Swan and taken to a farmhouse.

Meanwhile Ben Caunt had turned up in London from his training quarters with his uncle, Ben Butler and Turner, on the Monday afternoon and went to Tom Spring's Castle in Holborn. Ben was in high spirits, though remarkably thin. He had got rid of every ounce of superfluous flesh and was nothing but bone and sinew.

After dinner there, at which Tom Spring and the elite of the Fancy were present Ben Butler disposed of some two hundred colours on the usual terms - a guinea each if he won - nothing if he lost.

The party caught the four o'clock train for Wolverton and they proceeded, with Spring and other friends, putting up at the Cock at Stony Stratford, which was elected as Caunt's headquarters.

Newport Pagnell was full of the Nottingham division. The Swan (Tom Westley's) and all the other inns were filled to excess. In the evening Spring went to the Swan to meet Bendigo's friends to settle the place of battle. Bendigo wished to fight in Bucks; Spring had seen constables with warrants and wanted to take them to Oxfordshire, to Lillingston Level, where Deaf Burke and Nick Ward fought in 1840. There was a long disputation, but at last they agreed to toss. Jem Ward, for Bendigo, won and they chose Bedfordshire so it was arranged that the ropes and stakes should come on to Newport Pagnell in the morning early and a journey made thence to the battlefield.

The morning of the fight arrived and it was obvious even early on that it was going to be a very hot day.

When Jem Ward's party arrived, with the crowd who had been at Wolverton right behind them, minds were changed again and this time it was decided that Whaddon in Buckinghamshire, which was about ten miles away, would be the place.

Tom Oliver journeyed off with the ropes and stakes in a cart and with thousands already in the cavalcade that followed it must have been a very impressive sight.

It was still quite early when many of the crowd started out on their journey to Whaddon but already the sun was beginning to throw down an unusual amount of heat. With the majority having to 'toddle[28]' it they did not forget to

---

[28] Walk

make public their feelings of annoyance at the selection of a spot so far away in terms more expressive than polite.

After a trudge of about three hours, a suitable piece of ground was selected and the ring was pitched and brisk business was done in the sale of tickets ranging from one shilling to five shillings each.

There was quite a scene at the Cock between the two combatants as Bendigo, seeing Caunt at the window, swore he would pay him for all the trouble that had been given when they finally got into the ring.

A little later, just as Tom Spring, with Caunt and his supporters, were leaving the Cock at Stony Stratford, the chief constable appeared and told Tom that Whaddon was in Bucks and that the police were determined not to allow the fight in that county. Spring immediately sent off a messenger to notify all concerned that the fight had to be moved outside of Buckinghamshire.

When the messenger arrived and the situation became known to the crowd, the Nottingham roughs swore that they would not allow a move to be made and declared that the stakes and ropes should not be shifted. However, when it was pointed out that the two protagonists would not be arriving at Whaddon, they reluctantly permitted Oliver and his assistants to strike the stakes and once more started on the road to Sutfield Green.

The cursing and swearing is said to have been fearful, for the journey was some eight miles, the sun broiling hot and no refreshments to be had on the road. The irritated mass moved toward Oxfordshire and some, the majority in fact, went across country to save distance and the remainder in vehicles along the dusty road. Whilst the exasperated crowd was making its second pilgrimage, Bendigo, Merriman and his patrons arrived at Stoney Stratford, having left Newport Pagnell at 9 a.m.

Although this journeying about was exceedingly mortifying to many, it was a piece of good fortune to thousands who came down by the later morning trains to Stoney Stratford, for had not the delay occurred many would have had this journey for nothing. By now over five thousand people were present and many more still arriving and as much as a sovereign was being paid for a lift on the road, while many from sheer exhaustion had to fall out.

When the string of carriages, horsemen and pedestrians arrived at the final rendezvous the numbers had swollen to quite ten thousand representing all ranks from the blasphemous ruffian to the fashionably attired London Corinthian.

It was not until half past two that the ring was finally formed and it was decided to try and avoid as much confusion as possible by creating a large outer circle. However, the Nottingham roughs, who were there in great force with sticks, made an invasion into the ring and demanded money from everyone – even those who had already paid handsomely for a ring side seat and they drove back all those who would not buy Nottingham tickets. The disorder was terrific with the half-drunken, infuriated crowd cursing, fighting, thieving and yelling. Spring, who had provided tickets for the London men, had not yet arrived.

At precisely twenty past three, amidst deafening cheers from the ten thousand spectators the men entered the ring - Caunt first, attended by Molyneaux and Jem Turner acing as his seconds and his uncle Ben Butler having charge of the bottles. Nick Ward and Jack Hannan, Jem Ward and Jem Burn attended Bendigo. After cordially shaking hands they tossed for choice of corners. Caunt won and of course took the higher ground, with his back to the sun.

Spring, in compliance with the articles, produced Caunt's belt and handed it to Bendigo to show it was the genuine article. He buckled it on in bravado around his waist as to intimate that it would have a right to remain there after the fight was over and laughingly offered to bet Caunt £50 that he would win the fight. Caunt declined; he evidently did not appreciate Bendy's sense of humour. The belt was then handed to Jem Ward for safekeeping to await the result.

There was then a dispute about who should referee the fight. Names were suggested and rejected for the post of referee, for it certainly required an amount of courage to undertake so delicate an office to the satisfaction of so questionable a mob. At length George Osbaldeston ("t'Auld Squire") was named. He had, to avoid the crush, gone to his carriage but when he was told that without he came forward there would be no fight, he generously returned and accepted office.

With the men having completed their toilets, the colours were tied to the stakes. Bendigo's colours were blue with white spots while Caunt's consisted of bright orange, with a blue border and had the following inscription in a garter in the centre upon it: "Caunt and Bendigo, for £200 and the Championship of England, 9th September, 1845," surrounded by the words, "May the best man win."

All was now ready, "Time" was called amidst breathless silence and the two veterans toed the scratch.

THE FIGHT

Round 1:
Caunt threw himself into attitude erect and smiling, whilst Bendigo at once began to play round him, dodging and shifting ground in his usual style. Caunt let fly his left, but missed Bendigo who was active on his pins, retreated and chanced left and right; at last he crept in closer, then out again, till, watching his opportunity, he got closer and popped in a sounding smack with his left on Caunt's right eye. After a few lively capers he succeeded in delivering another crack with his left on Caunt's cheek, opening the old scar left by Brassey and drawing first blood, as well as producing an electric effect on Caunt's optic, producing shouts un-limited from Bendigo's friends. Bendy got away laughing and again played round his man. Caunt got closer, missed an intended slasher with his left and closed for the fall. Bendy grappled with him, but could not escape and Caunt, by superior strength, forced him down at the corner

Round 2:
Caunt up at the call of time, his cheek and eye testifying the effects of the visitations in the last round, Bendy dancing round him and waiting for an opening. Slight exchanges left and right, Caunt missing his opponent's head, Bendigo, in retreating to the ropes, slipped down, was up again in a moment and dashed to his man. Wild exchanges, but no apparent execution; Caunt hit out viciously left and right, missed his kind intentions and Bendy got down unscathed.

Round 3:
Caunt came up quiet and determined on annihilation. Bendy again played about him, but did not get near enough for execution. After some wild passes, Caunt missing, Bendigo, on the retreat, was caught in the powerful grasp of Caunt, who threw him across the ropes and fell on him, provoking plenty of shouts from the roughs - but no mischief done.

Round 4:
Caunt came up blowing, when Bendigo after a little dodging, popped in his left under his guard and got away. Caunt determined on mischief, followed his man and at last getting to him let fly left and right, catching Bendy with the left on the mouth slightly, but missing his right. Bendigo finding himself in difficulties got down, falling on the ropes and grinning facetiously at Goliath the Second, who walked back to his corner.

Round 5:
Caunt, first to lead off, drew on his man, but Bendy retreated, Caunt after him, till he reached the ropes, when Caunt hit out left and right, his blows passing harmlessly over Bendigo's head. There was a want of precision in Caunt's hitting not to be accounted for with his supposed science. Bendigo, who stopped rather wildly, got down.

Round 6:
Caunt, first to the call of time, waited with his hands well up, but blowing. He appeared to be over-trained and really distressed thus early in the struggle. Bendy manoeuvred to the right and left; Caunt approached him, but he retreated. Caunt let fly left and right, but Bendy ducked his canister and got down with more caution than gallantry.

Round 7:
Left-handed exchanges on the nobs but of no moment. Caunt made some desperate lunges left and right, but way too high and Bendy slipped down.

Round 8:
Bendy, after a few dodges, got within Caunt's guard with his left and gave him a pretty prop on the cheek. Caunt missed his return but, seizing Bendy in his grasp, flung him over the ropes. Here he leaned heavily on him, overbalanced himself and fell over on his own head, bringing Bendy with him, amidst loud shouts and abusive epithets. Caunt fell at the feet of his friends, Tom Spring and the editor of Bell's Life, the latter of whom was seated on that side of the ring near the centre stake.

Round 9:
Bendy came up full of glee and played round his man, watching for his opportunity to plant his left. This at last offered and catching Caunt on the old wound he ducked his head to avoid the return and got down.

Round 10:
More sly manoeuvring by Bendy, who after dancing about at arm's length, stole a march and caught Caunt a stinging smack with his left on the right cheek, drawing more claret and giving the Big 'Un more of the tragedy hue. Caunt instantly closed, gave Bendy one of his favoured hugs before throwing him to the ground and falling on him.

Round 11:
Bendy pursued his eccentric gyrations round his man, when with the swiftness of lightning he popped in his left on the jaw and right on the body and fell. Caunt, stung by the visitations, followed him and dropped on his knees close to his man, but luckily did not touch him and Bendy was picked up laughing and uninjured; in fact, up to this time he scarce showed the semblance of a hit beyond a slight contusion on the lip and left ear.

Round 12:
Bendigo retreated from Caunt's vigorous charge right and left and slipped down, but instantly jumped up and renewed the round after some wild fighting, but no execution worth recording, Bendy went down in his corner, amidst cries of "Foul", "Un-manly" &c.

Round 13:
Caunt, on coming to the scratch, let fly with his left, just grazing the top of Bendigo's scalp. A sharp rally followed and counter hits with the left were exchanged, Bendy hitting Caunt with such terrible force on the old spot on the right cheek that he knocked him clean off his legs, thus gaining the first knock-down blow, amidst deafening shouts from the Nottingham Lambs. Bendigo's blow was so powerful that he actually rebounded back against the stakes and Caunt was picked up almost stunned by the severity of the visitation.

Round 14:
Bendy, elated with his handiwork in the last round, again dashed in with his left, but not being sufficiently quick in his retreat Caunt caught him round the neck with his left and lifted him to the ropes and there hung on him till, in trying to escape from his grasp, he pulled him forward, threw and fell heavily on him, amidst the indignant shouts of his opponent.

Round 15:
Bendy came up as lively as a kitten, while Caunt, undismayed, came smiling to the scratch. Caunt plunged in his left and right, but missed, then seized his man for the throw, but Bendy slipped round and seizing Caunt by the neck pulled him down.

Round 16:
Bendy tried his left-hand dodge, but missed and retreated. Caunt followed him up to the corner, hitting out right and left, but throwing his hands too high. Caunt grappled for the fall but Bendy got down, Caunt following suit and as he sat upon the ground beckoned Bendy to come to him.

Round 17:
Bendy made himself up for mischief and played round his man for a few seconds, when, getting within distance, he delivered a terrific hit with his left on Caunt's mouth and fell. Caunt's upper lip was completely split by this blow and the blood flowed from the wound in torrents, producing renewed cheers from the Nottingham division. Bendy again came the artful dodge, put his left on Caunt's mouth and fell. Caunt pointed at him, but Bendy laughed and nodded.

Round 18: [no details]

Round 19:
Bendy, more cautions, kept out. Caunt rushed to him, hitting out left and right, but with little effect. Bendy retreated, Caunt caught him on the ropes and hung on him till he fell, producing more shouting and some threats at Caunt.

Round 20:
Caunt, anxious to be at work, advanced, while Bendy retreated to the ropes where he hit up with his left and slipped. Caunt turned his back and was retiring, when Bendy jumped up and had another slap at him. Caunt turned round and caught him under his arm as he attempted to escape, lifted him to the ropes and there held him till he fell, amidst the cries of Bendy's friends.

Round 21:
Caunt prompt to the call of time his hands well up, but Bendy again stole a march, popped in his left and slipped down to avoid a return of the

compliment. (Indignant expressions at Bendigo's shifty way of terminating the rounds.)

Round 22:
Bendy was still free from punishment and looked as fresh as when he entered the ring, while Caunt, although firm and active on his pins, showed heavy marks of punishment on his frontispiece, his cheek had a gaping wound, his lip cut and eye and nose evincing the consequence of Bendy's sly but stinging visitations. Caunt, impatient at Bendy's out-fighting, rushed to him left and right, but Bendy, unwilling to try the weight of superior metal, slipped down and Caunt fell over him, but not on him, as his friends anticipated and as perhaps he intended.

Round 23:
Both fresh. After a little dodging, advancing and retreating, Bendy again nailed Caunt with his left on his damaged kissing-trap. Caunt caught him a slight nobber on the head with his left and Bendy got down.

Round 24:
Bendy again played round his man till within distance, when he popped in a heavy blow on the ribs with his left and got down without a return. There was an immediate cry of "Foul" and an appeal was made to the referee. He hesitated, amidst tumultuous cries of "Fair", "Fair" and allusions to the size of Caunt. The uproar was terrific and the inner circle was overwhelmed by the roughs from without, rushing in to enforce their arguments in favour of Bendy. At last the referee decided "Fair" and "Time" was called.

Round 25:
Nick Ward was here so overcome with his exertions that he was taken out of the ring and his office was filled by Nobby Clark. The moment "Time" was called and Bendy reached the scratch, Caunt rushed to him left and right and after slight and wild exchanges with the left Bendy slipped and got down cunning.

Round 26:
Bendy, after a little hanky-panky manoeuvring popped in his left on Caunt's mug and retreated to the corner of the ring. Caunt followed him with so much impetuosity that he hit his hand against the stake. In the close and scramble for the fall, Bendy succeeded in pulling Caunt down, falling with him.

Squire Osbaldeston

Round 27: [no details]

Round 28:
Caunt attempted to lead off with his left, but Bendy retreated to the ropes, over which Caunt forced him and as he lay upon him, both still hanging on the lower rope, Bendy hit up with his left. In this position they lay, half in and half out of the ring, till released by their seconds.

Round 29:
Caunt let fly left and right, but he was short, Bendy playing the shifty game. Wild fighting on both sides, till Caunt fell on his knees. Bendy looked at him, lifted his hand to strike, but he prudently withheld the blow and walked to his corner to shouts from the Nottingham Lambs.

Round 30:
A rally, in which both fought wildly, Caunt catching Bendy a crack over the right brow, from which the claret flowed and Bendy returning the complement on Caunt's smeller. In the end Bendy slipped down and on rising, a small black patch was placed on the damaged thatch of his peeper

Round 31:
Bendy resumed his hitting and getting down system, popping in his left on Caunt's muzzle and slipping down.

Round 32:
The same game repeated. Spring, indignant, appealed to the referee at the way Bendigo was conducting the fight; and Molyneaux, in like manner, called on the umpires for their decision; they disagreed and Molyneaux ran to the referee. The roughs again had their say. A blow was aimed at Spring's head with a bludgeon, which fortunately only fell on his shoulder. It was a spiteful rap and he felt the effect of it for some days. The referee declared, however, that he had not seen anything unfair and Molyneaux returned to his man and brought him to the scratch at the call of "Time", amidst tremendous confusion, sticks in operation in all directions and many expressing great dissatisfaction at Bendy's unfair mode of fighting.

Round 33:
A short round, in which Bendy retreated and Caunt, following, caught him at the ropes and threw him over, falling on him.

Round 34 to 36:
Bendy again popped in his left and threw himself down. This was repeated in the two succeeding rounds, but Bendy's friends attributed it to accident and not design and there was no adverse decision on the part of the referee, whose position, amidst the tumult that prevailed, was far from enviable. He must have been possessed of no small nerve to have presumed to decide against the arguments that were so significantly shaken in the vicinity of his knowledge-box and to this must be attributed his reluctance to give a candid opinion.

Round 37:
Bendy tried his hit and get-down practice, bur Caunt seized him round the neck, threw and fell over him.

Round 38:
A wild and scrambling rally, in which Bendigo caught it on the nob. After a scramble they fell, Caunt within and Bendigo without the ropes, when each put his tongue out at the other like angry boys.

Round 39:
A slight exchange of hits with the left, when Bendy went down laughing.

Round 40:
Bendy popped in his left on Caunt's ancient wound, his right on the ribs and slipped down.

Round 41:
Bendy renewed his left-handed visitation and was retreating, when Caunt rushed after him, caught him at the ropes, over which he threw him and fell on him. A blow was here aimed at Caunt's head by one of the roughs with a bludgeon, but it fell on Bendy's shoulder.

Round 42:
Exchanges of hits left and right, when Bendy got down.

Round 43:
Bendy manoeuvred in his old way, delivered a smashing hit with his left on Caunt's throat and went down to avoid a return.

Round 44:
Caunt came up fresh and rushed to the assault, but Bendy got down. Caunt, indignant, jumped over him, but luckily fell on his knees beyond him, without touching him. It was assumed that he meant to jump on him and an uproarious appeal of "Foul" was made to the referee, who, after much confusion decided in the negative and ordered the men to go on.

Round 45:
Bendy renewed his manoeuvrings and tried his left, but Caunt seized him round the neck with his right and swung him twice round like a cat. Bendy succeeded in getting the lock with his right leg, when Caunt gave him a twist, threw and fell heavily on him, a little to the derangement of the Nottingham heroes, who shouted vociferously.

Round 46:
Caunt again succeeded in catching Bendy by the neck under his powerful arm, threw and fell heavily on him, but at the same time came with great force against the ground itself.

Round 47:
Caunt led off with his left, catching Bendy on the forehead. Bendy retreated, hit Caunt as he came in with his left on his distorted phiz[29], dropped and looked up in derision. Appeal from this species of generalship seemed now to be idle and was not repeated.

Rounds 48 to 57:
The succeeding ten rounds were fought in the same style. Little worthy of note occurred, each in turn obtained some trifling advantage in the hitting or failing but neither exhibited any disposition to say enough. It appeared that Bendigo, from his repeated falls, began to show signs of fatigue. The confusion round the ring continued most annoying, although the ropes and stakes were still preserved in their entirety. Many persons, from the pressure of those behind, were completely exhausted and happy to beat a retreat. The Editor of Bell's Life and friends were caught up in the confusion around the ring and complained that they had repeatedly to bear the weight of some half-dozen neighbours to which the bodies of both Caunt and Bendigo were occasionally added as they fell over the ropes onto them. During all this time the members of the London Ring with one or two exceptions (Macdonald and

---

[29] The face

Johnny Broome in particular), were perfectly quiescent and looked on with modest timidity, evidently afraid to interfere with the "club law" of the Nottingham bands who were regularly organised and obeyed the signals of their leaders with a discipline worthy of a better cause.

Round 58:
Bendigo 'jumped Jim Crow' around his man, tipped him a left-handed smeller and dropped without a return.

Round 59:
Caunt followed Bendy to the corner of the ring, hitting out left and right, but without precision and certainly without doing execution Bendy nailed him with his left in the old style and slipped down, but instantly jumped up to renew the round. Caunt, instead of stopping to fight, considering the round over, ran across the ring to his corner, Bendy after him, till they reached the ropes and after a confused scramble in which Bendy wed his left and right behind Caunt's back, both were down amidst general expressions of distaste at this style of fighting, but loud applause for Bendy

Round 60:
Caunt no sooner on his legs than to his man, but Bendy escaped his intended compliments left and right, threw in his left on the mouth and dropped, Caunt falling over him

Round 61:
One hour and twenty-four minutes had now elapsed but there were still no symptoms of an approaching termination to the battle; each appeared fresh on his pins and strong; although Caunt showed awful flesh wounds on his dial, there was nothing to diminish the hope of his friends. Bendy exhibited but a few slight contusions and although, no doubt, shaken by the falls and his own repeated prostrations, he appeared as active and leery as ever. Caunt, anxious to be at work, rattled to his man, hitting left and right, but Bendy retired and fell back across the ropes.

Round 62:
Bendy again on the retreat; Caunt after him, hitting wildly and without precision left and right. Bendy gave him upper pop with his left and slipped down. Caunt was retiring when Bendy jumped up again to renew active operations, but Caunt dropped on his knees, looked up in Bendy's face, grinning, as much as to say, "Would you?" and Bendy, deeming discretion the

better part of valour, contented himself with shaking his fist and retiring to his corner. Spring here remarked that jumping up to hit a man when the round was over and when he was unprepared, was as much foul as striking a man when he was down.

Round 63:
Caunt let fly left and right but missed his blows. Both slipped down on their knees in the struggle that followed and laughed at each other. In Caunt's laugh, from the state of his mug, there was little of the comic.

Round 64:
Bendy renewed his hanky-panky tricks and trotted round his opponent. Caunt rushed to him, but he retreated to the ropes, hit up and dropped but instantly rose again to renew the round. Caunt was with him, but he again got down, falling over the bottom rope and Caunt narrowly escaped dropping with his knee on a tender part.

Round 65:
Bendy again dropped his left on the sly on Caunt's damned phiz and went down. Caunt fell over him, jumped up and retired to his corner.

Round 66:
A slight rally, in which wild hits were exchanged and Bendy received a pop in the mouth, which drew the claret. Bendy dropped on one knee, but although Caunt might have hit him in this position, he merely drew back his hand and refrained.

Round 67:
Bendy came up cautious, keeping a good distance for a few seconds, when he slyly approached, popped in a tremendous body blow with his left and dropped, as if from the force of his own delivery, but evidently from a desire to avoid the return. Caunt winced under the effect of this hit and went to his corner.

Round 68:
Caunt quickly advanced to his work. but Bendy retreated to the corner, waited for him, popped in a light facer and, in a wild scramble, got down.

Round 69:
Bendy threw in another heavy body blow with his left and was going down when Caunt, with great adroitness, caught him round the neck with his left arm, lifted him completely off the ground and, holding him for a few seconds, fell heavily on him.

Rounds 70 to 73:
Scrambling rounds, in which wild exchanges took place and Bendy slipped down as usual to avoid punishment.

Rounds 74:
Caunt to the charge and Bendy on the retreat to the corner, where he succeeded in flinging in his left with terrific force on Caunt's damaged cheek and dropped.

Round 75:
Bendy again on the retreat, till he came to the ropes, over which he was forced, Caunt on him.

Round 76:
Caunt planted his left on Bendy's pimple and he slipped down.

Round 77:
A scrambling round, in which both hit wildly and without effect. Caunt in vain tried to nail his man with his right; he was always too high and Bendy went down. The uproar without the ring was tremendous and whips and sticks were indiscriminately applied.

Round 78:
Bendy, after some dodging, delivered his right heavily on Caunt's body and got down. It was a fearful smack.

Round 79:
Caunt led off with his left; Bendy ducked to avoid; and in the close both were down. Bendy was too cunning to allow his opponent the chance of the throw.

Round 80:
Bendy made his favourite sly hit with his left on Caunt's smeller and slipped down without the account being balanced. "Time" was very inaccurately kept, a minute, instead of half that time, being frequently allowed.

Round 81:
Bendy again displayed symptoms of fatigue and was tenderly nursed. On coming to the scratch, however, he planted his left on Caunt's carcase and slipped down.

Round 82:
Caunt led off. Bendy retreated to the ropes and fell backwards stopping, but instantly jumped up to recommence hostilities, when Caunt literally ran away across the ring, with his head down, Bendigo after him, hitting him on the back of his neck. At length Caunt reached his corner and in the scramble which followed and in which Caunt seemed to have lost his presence of mind, both went down, amidst contemptuous shouts at the imputed pusillanimity of the Champion.

Round 83:
Bendy, on the retreat, hit up; Caunt returned the compliment on Bendy's mouth with his left and on Bendy attempting to get down he caught him round the neck with undiminished strength, pulled him up, threw him over and fell heavily on him.

Round 84:
Bendy, on being lifted on his second's knee, showed blood from the mouth and was certainly shaken by the last fall; still he came up boldly, but cautiously Caunt rattled to him left and right, but he retreated towards the stake, which Caunt caught with his right as he let fly at him and Bendy slipped down, receiving a body tap as he fell.

Round 85:
Caunt rushed to his man, but Bendy, on his attempting to close, got down, unwilling to risk another heavy fall. He was obviously getting fatigued from his exertions and the excessive heat of the sun. The uproar was now greater than ever; the referee was driven into the ring and the roaring and bawling in favour of Bendigo in contempt of Caunt were beyond description. Once again the Editor of Bell's Life and their friends were overwhelmed in the confusion and were with difficulty extracted from a pyramid of our fellow men by the welcome aid of Jack Macdonald, their togs torn and their tile quite shocking. The exertions of Jem Ward and others enabled them to restore the referee to his position, but he was evidently in a twitter and the whips and sticks often reached within an inch of his castor, while they fell heavily on the nobs of

Ben Caunt and Bendigo

some of his neighbours. Several Corinthians who endeavoured to brave the storm, were involved in the general melee and had sufficient reason to be disgusted with the conduct of the parties towards whom they are always disposed to vouchsafe their patronage and who, with few exceptions, looked on inactive.

Round 86:
The Nottingham hero came up nothing daunted, but with an evident determination to continue to play the old soldier. Caunt, as usual, evinced a desire to get to his opponent, but the latter jumped away and waiting his opportunity threw in his left heavily on the Big 'Un's eye and, in escaping from the retort, slipped down.

Round 87:
Caunt, although so repeatedly hit, came up as fresh and strong as ever. He was incapable, however, of parrying the cunning dodges of Bendy, who again gave him a stinging rap on the cheek and, staggering back, fell, amidst cries of "Foul" and appeals from Caunt's friends to the referee; but in the din which prevailed no decision was obtained.

Round 88:
Two hours had now elapsed and still there was no apparent approximation towards a termination of the combat, while the confusion which prevailed round the ring prevented anything like a dispassionate criticism of the operations within. Bendy came up slowly, while Caunt was evidently disposed to annihilate him, as indeed his formidable fists induced everyone to believe he would have done long before, but Bendy prudently kept out of distance until a slight opening in the guard of Caunt enabled him to jump in and deliver his left twice in succession, on effecting which he slipped down and looked up with a triumphant leer at the mystified Champion.

Round 89:
Bendy again made himself up for mischief and, cleverly avoiding Caunt's attempt to reach him left and right, delivered a heavy hit with his right on the Champion's ribs which was distinctly heard amidst the row; after which he dropped and Caunt retired to the corner.

Round 90:
A close and struggle for the fall, which Caunt easily obtained, falling heavily on his adversary and his knee again happily escaped pressure on a vital part.

From Bendy's shifty tactics it was impossible for Caunt to avoid falling as he did. It, however, led to a fresh appeal by Johnny Hannan, on the part of Bendigo and a contradiction by Molyneaux on the part of Caunt. The umpires disagreed and the question having been put to the referee, amidst a horrible outcry raised by both parties, was decided "Fair" declaring that there was nothing intentional on the part of Caunt.

Round 91:
A scrambling round. A close, in which, after having delivered his left, Bendy contrived to get down, amidst fresh cries of "Foul" and "Fair".

Round 92:
Exchanges of hits with the left, when Bendy, stooping to avoid the repetition of Caunt's blow, as he was going down struck Caunt below the waistband and near the bottom of his stomach. Bendy fell on his back at the moment, while Caunt dropped his hands upon the place affected and fell as if in great pain. An indescribable scene of turmoil ensued; shouts of "Foul" and "Fair" escaped from "a thousand tongues - a thousand pair of iron lungs," many evidently influenced by their desires and not their convictions. There is no doubt that the blow, according to the rules of the Prize Ring was foul; but that it was intentional it is difficult to say, as it was struck when Bendy was in the act of falling. At last the umpires, disagreeing, made the customary appeal to the referee, who almost deafened by the roaring of the multitude, finally said he had not seen the blow and consequently could not pronounce it foul. The seconds immediately returned to their principals and the latter, "Time" being called, commenced the fight.

Round 93:
The men were quickly at the scratch and Caunt commenced operating left and right, catching Bendy slightly on the forehead. Bendigo was forced back upon the ropes almost in a recumbent position, but got up and was again knocked down and Caunt turned from him, considering the round had concluded. Bendy, however, awake to every chance of administering punishment, jumped up as he had done before and rushing after Caunt, who was half turned from him, was about to let fly when Caunt dropped on his nether end evidently disinclined to renew or continue round. And now a final and, as it turned out, a decisive appeal was made to the referee (not by the umpires but by Jem Ward, Hannan and others), who, with very little hesitation, pronounced the word "Foul" declaring that he considered Caunt had deliberately violated the rules of the Prize Ring by going down without a blow and had therefore lost

the fight. This verdict was hailed with the loudest vociferations by the roughs and Bendy, without further delay, was borne off the scene of his unexpected triumph by his partisans and carried to his carriage amidst reiterated acclamations.

The fight ended so suddenly that thousands in the crowd were for some time unable to discover who was the victor with many imagining that the foul blow in the previous round had led to the decision being against Bendigo. It was only by those immediately next to the ring that the true situation was known; the mortification and disappointment of the friends of Caunt, who stood up immediately afterwards to renew the fight, were beyond description. Caunt himself, as well as Spring and his seconds was incredulous as to the result.

They approached the referee, who had escaped from the rabble, but he left them in no doubt on the subject. He declared he had seen Caunt go down without a blow and that upon his conviction of the unfairness of such conduct he had pronounced against him. Spring remarked that there had been clearly an exchange of blows that to all appearance the round had been finished and that when Caunt went down he did so from a determination not to be taken by surprise or to renew the struggle till "Time!" was again called. The referee said he judged from what he saw in the overwhelming difficulties in which he was placed and he had given his decision accordingly. Both parties had agreed that he should be chosen to referee and he had accepted the office against his own inclination. In discharging his duty he had done so impartially to the best of his abilities and certainly had no bias in favour of one man or the other.

Caunt's followers were unhappy on a number of points. It was the duty of the referee to have withheld his decision till properly appealed to, not by the interested partisans, but by the appointed officials. The appointed officials were on the other side of the ring from him and could hold no immediate communication with him. He ought to have been placed between those persons. He was clearly bullied and hurried into a premature judgement. Had he been allowed to reflect for a while they were convinced he would have hesitated before pronouncing as he did in Bendigo's favour.

The time occupied by "the battle," was two hours and ten minutes.

On Bendy reaching his carriage, he was described as being 'dreadfully exhausted' both from the repetition of heavy falls to which he had been exposed as well as his own continued exertions on a very hot day. But his punishment being of comparatively a trifling description, he soon recovered on the application of proper restoratives. The only perceptible marks of the visitations of Caunt to his cranium were a cut over his right eye, a few contusions of the cheek, mouth, scalp and forehead and a little enlargement of his auricular organ. He was quickly conveyed from the ground to his quarters, both he and his friends highly elated at the result of their operations.

Caunt, on quitting the arena, although displaying convincing marks of the severity with which his opponent could use his mawleys, was strong on his legs, but dreadfully mortified at having been thus suddenly stripped of his laurels and deprived of the proud distinction, which he had so long held.

Spring who had throughout acted as his fidus Achates[30] was mentally depressed, not only from his incessant exertions to procure fair play throughout the fight and the cowardly assaults to which he was exposed, but also from a perfect conviction that the decision against his man was not only premature, but utterly opposed to the rules of the Prize Ring. He lost no time in returning with Caunt to the Cock, at Stony Stratford and the great event of the day having been concluded, the immense multitude followed suit.

The scenes exhibited on the road home were of the most extraordinary description. Every house of entertainment was besieged and the call for swizzle[31] so continuous that many of the best-filled cellars were exhausted and even water at last became an acceptable luxury to those who never pretended to be patrons of the hydropathic system.

The Editor of Bell's Life summarised the fight as follows:
"Upon the character of "the Great Fight for the Championship of England"; we have no doubt our readers have formed their own opinions. During the last thirty years it has been our fate to witness almost every important battle in the Prize Ring, but we confess, although we have occasionally had to record transactions of the most discreditable description and to administer castigation to wrong-doers in no measured terms, the proceedings on Tuesday far exceed in enormity anything we had before witnessed.

With regard to the pretensions of the two men who took so prominent a part in the day's proceedings few remarks are necessary. Caunt, although a big man

---

[30] A faithful friend
[31] Intoxicating drink

and possessed of great physical strength, does not possess the attributes of an accomplished boxer. He is deficient in science and wants the art of using the gifts of nature with that tact and precision, which are calculated to ensure success. There was a wildness and indecision in his deliveries which prevented his doing execution and the major part of his blows either flew over Bendigo's head or were short or wide of their destination. Had he been steady and self-possessed and hitting at points, this would not have been the case and did he understand the perfect art of self-defence, four-fifths of the punishment he received might have been avoided - but he left himself open to attack and thus his opponent was enabled to plant on him with stinging severity.

With a man of his own bulk the case might have been different and perhaps there are few, if any, of the present day that would prove superior to him in fair fighting.

Naturally there was great dissatisfaction at this verdict and Squire Osbaldeston was accused of having been intimidated by the Nottingham Lambs so much so that the stakeholder was served with legal notice by Spring to return the stakes. The referee (Osbaldeston) wrote thus to that gentleman via Bell's Life in London:

To the Editor of BELL'S LIFE IN LONDON.
SIR, an appeal having been made to me, as referee, by Mr. Spring, to reverse my decision in the late fight between Bendigo and Caunt, on grounds unworthy of my consideration, I request you will confirm that decision by paying over the stakes to Bendigo, who, in my opinion, is justly entitled to them. It was with the greatest reluctance and at the particular request of my friends and the unanimous solicitations of the backers of the men that I accepted the office; but I shall always consider it one of the greatest acts of folly I ever was guilty of in my life. In discharging my duty I endeavoured to do justice to the contending parties to the best of my abilities and judgment; and, arriving at the conclusion I did and now confirm, I was actuated only by a complete conviction of the justness of my decision and not by the intimidation of the roughs, as stated by Mr. Spring in his letter.

After some further remarks in reply to Spring, the referee goes on to say:

Had I been under the intimidation of the ' roughs ' I had several opportunities of putting an end to the fight before the conclusion by foul acts on the part of Caunt. A noble lord and several gentlemen, who stood close by me during the whole fight, can corroborate this statement. I most positively deny that I stated to anyone that a man going down without a blow, after he himself had treacherously delivered blows, was fair. In no one instance, in my judgement, did Bendigo break the laws of fair fighting. I must also deny, in the most positive manner that I ever stated to any person that I did not see the last round. I saw every round distinctly and clearly and when Caunt came up the last round he had evidently not recovered from the 92nd. After the men were in position Bendigo very soon commenced operations and Caunt turned round directly and skulked away, with his back to Bendigo and sat down on his nether end. He never knocked Bendigo down once in the fight, nor ever got him against the ropes in the last round. In my opinion Caunt got away as soon as he could from Bendigo, fell without a blow to avoid being hit out of time and fairly lost the fight.

I am, your obedient servant,
THE OLD SQUIRE.
Doncaster, Sept. 18th, 1845.

So William Thompson, better known as Bendigo became for the second time Champion of England.

As a final note on this fight George (or Squire) Osbaldeston (1787-1866) led a life filled with sporting feats including shooting, riding with the Quorn Hunt, cricketer, riding 200 miles in a record time of less than nine hours, etc., etc...

Encouraged by his wife, he wrote his life story in 1856, his seventy-first year and completed it on October 10th 1862 and having no children with his wife Elizabeth he presented the documents to his wife's son Mr John Williams. As the years passed Mr Williams in turn passed them to his son Mr G. H. Williams of Chippenham.

Mr G. H. Williams showed the documents to Mr G. D. Armour and then to Mr. E. D. Cuming who edited the documents and ensured a book entitled Squire Osbaldeston His Autobiography was published in March 1926.

It appears that in the original document, pages were missing from Chapter XIV and page 263 of the Squire's autobiography edited by E. D. Cuming has the following comment:

"The pages missing from Chapter XIV may have borne an account of another Championship fight at which Osbaldeston was referee: that between Ben Caunt and Bendigo (Wm Thompson) at Sutfield Green, Oxfordshire on 9th September, 1845. This battle was very stoutly contested, the men fighting for two hours. In the 93rd round the Squire gave his decision in favour of Bendigo on the ground that Caunt had deliberately violated the Rules of the Prize Ring by going down without a blow. This verdict was sharply criticised; it was urged that Bendigo had gone down numbers of times to avoid punishment, without objection: and Osbaldeston's decision was attributed to fear of the Nottingham "Lambs" who surrounded the ring."

So why were the pages covering the Caunt/Bendigo fight missing? Who had removed them? Had the Squire written admitting to favouring Bendigo? Had he later changed his mind and removed the pages himself? Had someone wanting to protect his good name removed them later?

Clearly we will never know the truth – but an interesting postscript to the fight all the same.

Chapter 9

THE FIRE AT THE COACH AND HORSES

(1851)

A terrible catastrophe, in which the champion suffered a heavy domestic bereavement, occurred during Caunt's temporary absence from London on a visit to some country friends in Hertfordshire. A fire broke out at Caunt's inn, The Coach and Horses on St Martin's Lane and two of Caunt's children, Martha and Cornelius and the servant (Mrs Caunt's niece), Ruth Lowe, who looked after the children, were burnt to death.

Ben did not return from the country until the following morning. Both he and his wife were completely inconsolable and deeply affected by the event.

The event was covered in detail by The Times newspaper as follows:

<u>16th January 1851</u>

FIRE AND LOSS OF LIFE IN ST. MARTIN'S LANE

Yesterday morning, shortly after 2 o'clock, a fire broke out at the Coach and Horses public house, St. Martin's Lane, the consequences of which have been most disastrous, three persons, respectively aged 13, 10 and 6 having fallen victims to the flames. The house was kept by the well known Ben Caunt, the pugilist and ex-champion of England and two of the deceased parties are his children, the third being a relative of Mrs. Caunt.

The building was three stories high and had three rooms on each floor. In the attics slept three children, together with the deceased Ruth Lowe, Edward Noakes, a waiter and Samuel Lowe, the potman, the latter being another cousin of Mrs. Caunt. The second floor front room was occupied by Mrs. Caunt; the middle room contained a spare bed and in the third or back room slept the nurse, Betsy Butler, with an infant child of Mrs. Caunt's.

Mr. Caunt had left town on Tuesday afternoon for Lewisham, on a shooting excursion and Mrs. Caunt, having closed the house, about 2 o'clock yesterday morning proceeded to retire to rest. Before doing so, she requested a niece, who was staying with her on a visit and who had hitherto occupied the second floor spare room, to sleep with her that night, as Mr Caunt was absent. The young woman consented and went into her room to fetch her night-dress, taking opportunity, at the request of her aunt, to examine the apartment and look under the bed to see that no one was concealed in the house. She had a candle in her hand while thus engaged and their appears reason to fear that an accidental spark falling upon some combustible material in this room must have occasioned the catastrophe.

Mrs. Caunt had been in bed only a very few moments when she was aroused by the waiter, Edward Noakes, calling out from the third floor that the house was on fire and urging his mistress to make her escape. Mrs Caunt roused her niece instantly and hastening out of her own room, went to the middle room for the purpose of alarming the nurse, who was sleeping with her infant in the back room. As soon as she opened the door of the middle room Mrs Caunt was nearly overpowered by the flames and the smoke with which the room was filled. With great intrepidity, however, she rushed forward and forcing open the door of the third room, called to the nurse to bring out her child. The nurse, perceiving her danger in an instant, did not stop to dress herself, but snatched up the child and followed Mrs. Caunt out of the room, literally walking through the flames, with which the apartment was filled.

Meantime Noakes, the waiter, had opened the trap door in the roof and was handing the persons who slept in this part of the house on to the leads and thence down through a skylight into the adjoining dwelling. The barmaid, the maidservant and Mr. Caunt's eldest son (a boy about 12 years of age), were all rescued in this manner and placed in safety by Noakes, who returned to look for the other children, but unfortunately too late to save them.

It appears that in their alarm and excitement they had got out of the bed and hidden themselves beneath it and it was here when the fire was got under control that the Brigade men found their remains burnt almost to a cinder. The body of Ruth Lowe, a remarkably fine young woman, aged 18, was found in another part of the room extended on the floor and reduced to an almost shapeless mass.

There was very little time lost in reducing the fire after the engines were got to work and the extent of damage done to the house is comparatively trifling.

The escape of the Royal Society for the Preservation of Life from Fire stationed near St. Martin's Church was early on the spot, but not sufficiently so to render essential service. Moreover, a portion of the machinery by which it is raised was accidentally broken by the wheel of a cab just as it was about to be applied to use.

The bodies have been removed to St. Martin's Workhouse, where the inquest will be held this day.

17th January 1851

THE FATAL FIRE IN ST. MARTIN'S LANE

Mr Bedford, the coroner, held an inquest at half-past 2 o'clock yesterday, at St. Martin's Workhouse, on the bodies of Ruth Lowe, Cornelius Caunt and Martha Caunt who were destroyed by fire on Wednesday morning in the Coach and Horses public house, St. Martin's Lane, kept by Benjamin Caunt, the ex-champion of England.

The jury having been sworn proceeded to view the bodies, which presented a most appalling spectacle - the limbs mangled and disfigured, the entrails protruding and their whole frames presenting a blackened and frightful aspect. The following witnesses were then called:-

Ann Tomlin, of 51, Castle Street said - I am wife of Richard Tomlin, licenced victualler. I knew the deceased, Ruth Lowe and Cornelius and Martha Caunt and I identify the bodies shown to me here as theirs. Ruth Lowe appeared to me to be about 18 years of age. She was a single woman and a servant. Cornelius Caunt was about six and his sister about eight. Their parents names are Benjamin and Martha Caunt. I was not on the premises and cannot tell any of the facts relating to the accident.

Susannah Thorpe - I live at 5, Kensington Park Road, Notting Hill. I went to Mr. Caunt's in the afternoon of Tuesday. I am a relation of Mrs. Caunt's. I was there when an alarm was given shortly after 2 o'clock in the morning. Mrs Caunt and myself were in the bar when the clock struck 2 and we went to bed shortly after. The three deceased persons went to bed some hours before. They all slept in one of the attics. I saw them when they were going to bed. The servant was sober and apparently well. Mr. Caunt was not at home and I slept with Mrs Caunt. When we had got into bed the manservant gave the alarm. We had not put out the light. Mrs. Caunt had not got into bed but I had. The barman came and alarmed us. Mrs Caunt immediately ran downstairs. We saw fire in the middle room. We lay in the front room on the second floor immediately under the others. The deceased were in the room above us. We saw smoke and fire in the middle room on the floor in which we slept. I don't know if there was a fire in the room where the deceased lay. I did not see the deceased taken out. The barman had gone to bed. There were no other persons occupying the attics that night. I suppose the fire broke out in the middle room on the second floor. A servant and the baby were in an adjoining room, there was no fire in either of these two rooms. I cannot identify how the fire originated. The barman slept in one of the attics. There are three rooms on each floor. The barman went into the room where the girl and the baby were sleeping. I don't know much about the house or its arrangements. Mrs Caunt and myself ran down to give the alarm. We were very much frightened.

Edward Noakes, cellarman to Mr. Caunt - I had been in bed about a minute and a half, before the alarm of fire was given. I slept in the back attic. I had no candle when I went up to bed; there was no fire in the room. I lit a candle after I got up and put it out before I went to bed. I smelt smoke immediately after getting into bed. I heard no noise. I sat up in bed and bellowed to Mrs. Caunt if she was lighting a fire. I got out of bed and she said, "No; the house is on fire." I then ran down stairs and saw the fire in the middle room. Two beds were on fire in the room. I went through the room into the other room and found that the nurse and baby had gone downstairs. There was no fire in any other room but the middle room. There was no fire in the room where the nurse and baby were, but there was smoke in it. I knew the deceased were sleeping in the attic adjoining when I slept there. I ran up stairs again and woke a man who was sleeping in my room and the deceased. I could not see them, but I could feel and hear them, though the smoke was so great that I could not see them. Three of the children generally slept in the same attic. The little boy Ben called out, "Here is the window;" and I then went to it and I got him out on the tiles and the barmaid and myself as well. The floor was not then burning, but the room was full of smoke. The three of us got over the tiles to the next house. I did not return to the room again and could not. On getting out I saw the fire escape in the street, but could not get to it. The fire originated in the middle room. I have nothing else to say.

(In response to questions by the jury) - The potman slept in the same room with me and he got out of the window. No one slept in the middle attic. We got out at the front window and passed through the room occupied by the deceased. Ruth Lowe was cook. The barman, barmaid, myself and one of the children escaped. Mrs Caunt and the witness Thorpe ran down stairs. I thought the deceased had escaped. They did not cry out. I heard no alarm from the street before I discovered the fire inside, but I heard Mrs. Caunt crying out "Fire" at the street door.

Dominick Carr, police sergeant F15 - I was on duty in St. Martin's Lane and passed by the Coach and Horses about three minutes before the alarm of fire was given, about 15 or 18 minutes past 2. At that time there was no symptom of a fire. I met the constable on duty and returned back again in about three minutes and turned up New Street, when I heard a woman cry out "Fire" and "Police." I ran back and at the corner of the street found the constable running and springing his rattle. Mrs Caunt was on the pavement, crying out for her children and that the house was on fire. I went inside the door, but could see no fire or smoke. Three constables came up and I sent for the engine and fire escape. I ascended the staircase. Mrs Caunt attempted to follow, but I ordered the constable to prevent her. I ascended and when I reached the landing on the first floor I heard the crackling of the flames. I went to the second floor and saw that the back part of the house was all in flames. On the second floor front I found the bed clothes down. The fire was in the adjoining room. I asked where the children were and they roared out "Higher up". I attempted to get up the staircase, but could not. I was nearly suffocated. It was impossible to get to the attics. I did not see or here anyone above. I then got down and the fire escape arrived about three minutes after I first entered the house. The fire escape was placed against the window on the second floor, but I ordered them to put it to the top of the house. Up to this time there was no cry from the top of the house. I got up on the adjoining house and I saw the fireman at the attic window. He broke the window and the flames rushed out and he said it was impossible to render assistance. The barman was not sober when I saw him. He was drunk. The only possibility of saving the children was from the top of the house. I saw the deceased taken out from the top attic, where the fireman attempted to get in. It was unfortunate the men had not remained on the roof. The fire must have originated from the middle room on the second floor.

(In response to questions by the jury) - I can't say that the children would have been saved if the fire escape had been put to the right window at first. The floor of the attic where the deceased were found was not much burnt.

A juryman stated that it was seven minutes after the alarm was given before a policeman came.

The witness and several of the jury said that was not true.

Some of the jury here volunteered versions of their own, contradictory of each other and of the testimony of the witnesses.

Ford Girrard, a fireman - I was called to the fire about 25 minutes past 2. I went up to Caunt's house and on entering it found I could not get up beyond the second floor back room. I then came down and got the hose up the staircase and commenced working the engine. The staircase leading up to the attics was gone. We got into the attics about 20 minutes after we commenced working and hearing that two children were lost a search was made for them and they were found. Some of the tiles had fallen in. The fire had gone up the staircase and not through the ceiling. The floor was not burnt through. The windows down stairs were open, which was a great help to the fire. The fire originated in the second floor back; but how it originated I cannot tell, nor do I think anyone else can. One of the children was half under the bed and the other was close by.

Sarah Barker - I am barmaid to Mr. Caunt. - I went to bed at half-past 11 on Tuesday night. I slept in the front attic with the deceased girl. Three children slept in the same room. I heard Mrs. Caunt cry out "Fire." I got out of bed and lifted the three children out of bed, but saw nothing more of them and thought they went downstairs. The cellarman was quite sober then. I saw no fire in the attic, but there was a great deal of smoke.

Charles Latham, fireman - I went to the house with the fire engine. I entered the house and found it was impossible to get beyond the second floor. I made search for the bodies. I first found the skull of the boy; the other part of the body was under the bed. The bodies were buried under what fell from the roof. The fire commenced in the second floor back.

John Short - I was called to Caunt's house and put the machine to the window of the second floor, as I was told there were children there. I went in and tried to get into the back room, but could not. I then put the machine to the attic and broke the window, but could not get in from the volume of the flames.

This closed the evidence and the jury returned a verdict – 'that the deceased had come by their death from fire, but that there was no evidence as to how the fire originated.'

18th January 1851

TO THE EDITOR OF THE TIMES
Sir, - In the name of London's 2,000,000 inhabitants, let me intreat of you, while breathing time and space are yet allowed by the Parliamentary recess, to say one word in favour of a suggestion to which from time to time you have given place in your columns, with the object of rescuing those whose lives are endangered by the sudden night fire.

The police sergeant Dominick Carr, whose evidence is recorded in The Times of today, says with reference to the poor suffocated children of St. Martin's Lane, that "the only possibility of saving them was from the top of the house;" and again, that it was a "a pity that the barman (who escaped from the window of the very room where they were burnt) had not remained upon the roof." To the roof of the burning house from that of the adjoining one did Carr at last, of himself and without orders, make his way; but too late to save three whose "roar for help," loud above the roar of the flames, he had heard some minutes before, in his courageous, though fruitless attempt, to ascend the staircase of the burning house. Let me, Sir, recall to the readers of The Times a suggestion which nearly seven years ago found place in its columns:-

"That immediately on the alarm of fire being given, it be a standing positive order to the policemen (one or more) who arrive on the spot, to make their way, without a moment's delay, to the roofs of the adjoining house, there to afford every help to the inmates of the burning house as circumstances may allow."

To the letter bearing the signature of 'M. D.' in The Times of April 10, 1844, in which this suggestion occurs and also two others from the same hand in The Times of respectively December 24, 1844 and May 30, 1845, I may refer as proofs of your never tiring readiness to promote the public good. Allow me again to quote the first letter of 'M. D.' as bearing most practically on this last sad event:-

"Were it generally known throughout London to householders and their families, that on the instant of an alarm of "Fire" being sounded through the street, two, if not more, well disciplined, resolute, able bodied men were fast making their way to the roofs of the houses on either side of the one on fire, there would surely be less of the panic and bewilderment which so often mar their efforts to escape. The lusty shout of a manly voice the gripe, it might be, of a well nerved hand, would cheer and resuscitate the half suffocated child or woman, otherwise fast sinking in despair. . . . . . The Londoners have now in their new police the best possible machine for the protection of life from fire. For God's sake act in the true spirit of city brotherhood, let them learn at once how to use it."

You, Sir, have already, by the space allowed to 'M. D.'s' letters, made this matter your own. With the more confidence do I again intreat you to speak yourself, as The Times knows how to speak and so, perhaps, to save many lives from being lost, many hearts from being broken by the awful havoc of a London fire.
I am, Sir, your very faithful servant.
London, Jan. 17 NEMO.

<u>18th January 1851</u>

THE LATE FIRE IN ST. MARTIN'S LANE

<u>TO THE EDITOR OF THE TIMES</u>
Sir, - In your report of the inquiry held yesterday at St. Martin's workhouse upon the bodies of the poor children and servant who lost their lives in the fire at the Coach and Horses, St. Martin's lane, you state, in the evidence of the sergeant of police, F 15, that the barman was intoxicated. This statement I allow he made, but it was contradicted by subsequent evidence. I, being one of the jurymen, elicited from the sergeant, before the coroner, that he did not see the barman for an hour after the fire commenced. I was in conversation with him immediately after his escape and at intervals for several hours after, during which time he was perfectly sober and well conducted; indeed, he carried with him the sympathies of the court and jury for his manly bearing all through the dreadful scene; and the coroner, in summing up, clearly stated that the imputation of the sergeant was satisfactorily contradicted and so far from any reproach resting upon him it appeared that he acquitted himself in a most unexceptionable manner. I, who know of an altercation that occurred in my house between this sergeant and the barman, can perfectly understand why he charged him with being drunk. Assured that I have only to name these facts to claim your notice of them.

I am, Sir, your obedient servant,
57, St. Martin's lane, Jan. 17. T. W. MARSHALL.

The following verse is from a book entitled 'Songs'. It was written at the time of the fire and is now part of a collection of songs and verses by various authors, which have been bound into one collection by the British Library.

ON THE AWFUL FIRE AT B. CAUNT'S
IN SAINT MARTIN'S LANE

That took place on Wednesday last, by which the lives of two of Mr. Caunt's children and the servant girl, niece to Mrs. Caunt, were lost.

I will unfold a tale of sorrow,
List, you tender parents dear,
It will thrill each breast with horror,
When the dreadful tale you hear.

Early on last Wednesday morning,
A raging fire as we may see,
Did occur, most sad and awful,
Between the hours of two and three.

Two pretty babes and servant maid,
Was burnt to death, how sad to name!
At Mr. Caunt's, the Coach and Horses,
Situate in St. Martin's Lane.

Benjamin Caunt his wife and children,
Left at home in health and bloom,
When he went out, little expecting,
They would meet such an awful doom.

In sweet repose they silent slumbered,
On their soft and downy beds,
But oh! Alas! Their days were numbered,
Now they sleep among the dead.

Dreadful was the fire raging,
The tender mother loud did call,
Nothing could be her grief assuaging,
Her pretty babes in death did fall.

And the servant maid who nursed them,
What a dreadful sight to see.
Can you imagine tender parents,
What must the mother's feelings be.

And oh! Again, pray mark the sequel,
When the father did the tidings hear,
For awhile he was bereft of reason,
Down his cheeks ran floods of tears.

He almost was drove to distraction,
He beat his breast and tore his hair,
Crying, Fire, that cruel tyrant,
Has robbed me of my children dear.

We cannot tell what lays before us-
Those pretty babes and nurse in bloom,
Was sudden snatched from among us,
And hurried to the silent tomb.

May God receive their souls in glory,
And dry up the parent's tears,
Grant them every consolation,
Since they have lost their children dear.

No more their smiles they'll be beholding,
No more their pretty faces see,
No more to their bosoms will they fold them,
Oh! What must their feelings be?

Numbers to the spot do hasten,
The sad place for to behold,
Sympathise each feeling Christian,
When the dreadful tale is told.

Benjamin Caunt was England's Champion,
By all respected was his name,
The landlord of the Coach and Horses,
Well known in St. Martin's Lane.

This dreadful fire so fierce was raging,
Between the hours of two & three o'clock,
On that fatal Wednesday morning,
Which has caused this dreadful shock.

Chapter 10

FAMILY SQUABBLE WITH NAT LANGHAM

(1852-1861)

The final appearance of Ben in the Prize Ring was one that adds no credit at all to the career of the ex champion. Some absurd family quarrels with Nat Langham, who had married Mrs. Caunt's cousin, together with some petty trade jealousy resulted in the two men ending up in the ring to settle their differences.

After his defeat by Bendigo in 1845, Ben declared that he should like to meet him for a fourth time. He was willing to put down between £500 and £1,000 on the condition that they should fight upon a raised platform to ensure that the ruffians could not get at the combatants. He also wanted the battle to take place a sufficient distance from the Nottingham Lambs to preclude their presence. But it all fell through and as time passed by he was looked upon as being on the shelf as far as prize-fighting was concerned. Although he still talked about fighting, however and would not admit that he was on the retired list.

Meanwhile, he was doing excellent business at his pub, the Coach and Horses in St. Martin's Lane. Ben was no fool. Although but a simple countryman, he was as sharp as a needle in looking after business and was a most genial host, until the misfortune of the fire happened to him that all but turned his brain and altered his disposition entirely, transforming him from a jovial host to an irritable man, who easily lost his temper and was not always answerable for what he said and did.

Ben was never the same man after that horrendous incident and it was this misfortune that undoubtedly led him to enter the lists again, for the irritability of his temper brought about the quarrel with Nat Langham.

Nat was related by marriage to the Caunts, the wives of the two men being cousins. But there was very little affection between the two ladies, who were always giving vent to ill temper and sarcastic remarks about each other's husband, for there were petty jealousies founded on Caunt's greater success in business.

If Ben had been left to himself no doubt they would have made it up but his wife was always calling attention to the way that Nat was carrying on the Cambrian Stores close by and declared that he was doing all he could to take the custom away from the Coach and Horses. Nat at times was a most provoking fellow, with a sarcastic tongue and a wit that brought him many admirers. He would to Ben Caunt's face tell him that he never could fight and that should they ever stand up together he could not hit him in a month of Sundays.

All this rankled with Caunt, but what put the finishing touch to the whole affair was the presence of Ben's uncle, old Ben Butler, who resided with them. He had become a disagreeable, sour old man, sitting in the bar parlour drinking his blue ruin and grumbling and swearing all day long, boasting that it was he who had brought out his nephew and that it was all through him that Ben had made his pugilistic successes and had been enabled to take the tavern in which he was doing such good business. Be that as it may, it is certain that old Ben Butler helped him a great deal and never missed one of his fights, whilst he always trained him and gave him the best advice, so Caunt had a great deal of faith in the old man. Little wonder, then, with Butler and his wife always nagging him and declaring that Nat Langham was his worst enemy, he should form a dislike to the celebrated middle weight.

Nat went to the Coach and Horses one morning in 1857 and commenced in his usual style to chaff Big Ben. The latter turned round and exclaimed, "Sitha, laad, th' art allus sayin' as tha can lick me and as I can't hit thee in a month o' Sundays. Well, naw I'll give thee a chance o' showin' whether tha can do what tha says. Coover these ten pun' " and he slapped down upon the counter two five pound notes " coover yon and I'll fight thee for as much as thou loikes, for nowt but a feight will work my ill blood off."

Nat was considered the best middleweight of his day and had a fine record, which included being the only man to record a victory over champion Tom Sayers. He was born in Hinckley in Leicestershire where he worked as a farm labourer, which helped to keep him fit for his early local fights. Later he moved to London to work briefly as a deliveryman and hone his skills under the direction of non other than the former heavyweight champion Ben Caunt.

Nat Langham

After the fight with Tom Sayers, Langham retired from boxing to open the Cambrian Stores, a tavern. He also owned a boxing booth and founded the Rum-Rum-Pas Club for aristocratic ring patrons.

At 37 years of age and although six years younger than Ben, Nat Langham, was, like Caunt, getting on in years for a pugilist and furthermore he was suffering from weak lungs, having been attending the Hospital for Consumption at Brompton.

Everybody was surprised when they heard that it looked like serious business, for here was Nat Langham, who belonged to the middle weights, accepting the challenge of an ex-champion and one of the biggest men who had ever won the Champion's belt.

The articles were formulated on the 16th of May, 1857, by which and a deposit of £10 a side, the parties agreed to stake £200 a side in instalments, the battle to come off on the 23rd of the ensuing September.

Deposit after deposit was punctually put down and the bitterness between them increased apace.

Ben Butler very nearly made a mess of it for his nephew, whilst the latter was away in Brighton. On May 11th, 1857 the men had affixed their signatures to the articles, which provided that they should fight for £200 a side, on September 23rd. Langham happened to be going out of town before the second deposit fell due, so he sent the 'tenner' in good time before the date that it was due. Old Ben Butler protested that it was not in accordance with the strict wording of the articles and on behalf of his nephew proceeded to claim the first deposit put down. This was a paltry bit of business and directly Caunt, who was away in Brighton, heard of it he wrote to Bell's Life the following letter:-

MR EDITOR, - I respectfully ask that you will admit into your columns this declaration on my part: That my match with Langham is the result of a dispute that can only be settled, so far as I am concerned, by an appeal to the fists. That the articles will be strictly abided by on my own part and that so far from throwing any impediment in the way of the match it is my anxious desire to bring it to an issue in the Ring. Thus far, I beg my friends will take my assurance of 'honourable intentions.' Were they but aware of the personal nature of the affair, such assurance would not be needed; but,

as many must necessarily be unacquainted with its cause of origin, it is due to my own character to take the course I have now done in writing to you an emphatic statement of my intentions, which I solemnly assert are unalterable, until that result comes to pass which shall prove either me or my antagonist the better man.
Yours, &c., BENJAMIN CAUNT.
Coach and Horses, St. Martin's Lane, London, May 27th, 1857.

To which the editor adds:-

"Ben has also paid us a personal visit and repeated the statements contained in his letter and in addition has given up all claim to the forfeit, which, from the first, we believe was not his own doing."

The atmosphere thus cleared, all went on serenely, the bona fides of the match, which had been sorely doubted and even ridiculed in sporting circles, being now placed beyond dispute.

In the June of 1857, Tom Sayers had defeated the Tipton Slasher in a battle for the Championship and the belt, which was a surprising result for the sporting world, when the weights of the two men were considered. Until then nobody had dreamed of matching an 11 stone man of medium height against a 14 stone man, standing over six feet.

This upset of the weights had an effect on Ben Caunt and he caused the following to appear in Bell's Life:

To the Editor of BELL'S LIFE IN LONDON

SIR, - Unaccustomed as I am to public challenging, long laid upon the shelf as I have been, it may perchance startle the sporting world to learn that Ben Caunt is once more a candidate for the Championship. Win or lose with Langham, I challenge Tom Sayers for £200 a side and the Championship, the contest to take place within six months of my forthcoming fight. My money is ready at your office and I trust that this offer will be accepted, in order that the world may be as speedily as possible undeceived with regard to the merits of the much-vaunted new school of British Boxing.
Yours obediently, BENJAMIN CAUNT.
June 18th, 1857.

With this letter was left the sum of £10 with the editor, so there was no doubt about Ben being actually in earnest. Tom Sayers was away on tour, making a lot of money in the provinces after beating the Slasher; so when Caunt wanted to have the articles signed at the Coach and Horses (of course the host looking at the custom this would bring him), Sayers declined, but said that he would send the deposit and sign, if the articles were sent to him but this did not suit Ben and after a deal of letter writing the whole thing fell through.

In May Ben announced his departure for 'sea breezes and strict training,' and Nat did the same.

Caunt had, during the twelve years he had been idle, naturally put on a good deal of superfluous flesh and weighed considerably over seventeen stone, so it was necessary for him to get into training in ample time, for to fight Langham it was considered that he should be as near 14st. as possible. So, in May, four months before the date set down for the battle he commenced gentle exercise by going down every day to the White Bear, Kensington and there played quoits for hours. Then he went to Ramsgate with Job Cobley, who was at the time matched to fight Bob Brettle. Caunt was a fine swimmer, so he took plenty of exercise in the sea and long walks in the bracing fresh air, whilst he did daily practice with the gloves. After being at Ramsgate, old Ben Butler appeared upon the scene and it was thought better to go to the quieter and more secluded Saltpan Sandwich; so they took a place for a month and did much about the same exercise. At the expiration of this period they came nearer to town, putting up at the Greyhound Inn, at Hatfield, near Woodside, in Surrey and Ben made wonderful progress for an old 'un.

Nat Langham, who really wanted to pick up strength rather than waste, went to Dover, in company with Frank Widdows, who came from Norwich, a comical character and just the sort of companion to have on such an excursion, for he was the life and soul of every convivial party and a favourite with all. Langham declared that Widdows was worth a dozen other trainers, for he could keep his man in the highest spirits with his inexhaustible fund of anecdotes, songs and jokes.

As to Nat's training, he went first to Dover and then to Stockbridge, in Hampshire, where by steadiness and perseverance he got himself into extraordinary fettle and he looked bigger, stronger and healthier, though of course somewhat older, than when he fought either Harry Orme or Tom Sayers.

The match, from its first inception, was considered so extraordinary, not only from the great disparity in the size of the men, but from the supposed irreparable state of Nat's constitution (he having, as was known to many, sought the advice of the principal physician of the Brompton Hospital for Consumption), that the public generally looked upon it with distrust and suspicion and up to the very last deposit sporting men refused to believe that it would ever come to a fight. Indeed, so strong was this impression on the minds of many and not a few of them influential patrons of the PrizeRing that they pooh-poohed the whole affair, absented themselves from the houses where deposits were made good.

The views held by the Fancy appeared to hold but two opinions on the subject. Either one or the other of the men would be apprehended and held to bail, or there would be police interference on the day. There was a general feeling of distrust and an awaited expectancy of the bursting of the bubble. Up to the eleventh hour this or some other obstacle was confidently predicted.

On the Monday, however, it was known that arrangements had been agreed on by Dan Dismore on the part of Nat Langham and Jemmy Shaw and Ben Butler on the part of Ben Caunt, to hire two steamboats between them, one for first and the other for second-class passengers. It was also arranged that the boats should rendezvous at Tilbury and that the men and their friends should proceed to the same place by the 7.50 a.m. train on the eventful morning.

In the course of Monday, however, it seems that apprehensions arose in the minds of Nat's friends that it would be unsafe to start from Tilbury and they telegraphed to the owner of the boats to change the venue and muster at Southend. They did not seem to think it necessary to communicate with Caunt or his uncle, concluding of course that they would be at the London terminus at the time arranged and that then everything could be settled.

At the time appointed Ben Butler and Young Ben (Caunt's son) were at Fenchurch Street, but Caunt did not show and it was thought of course he had adopted some other means of conveyance. At Tilbury, however, Uncle Ben and Jemmy Shaw said that Caunt expected the boat at Tilbury and had

Nat Langham

not heard of any alteration. Here again suspicions arose that some casualty had happened and that there would be no fight. Ben's friends could give no reason for his not being at the appointed station in the morning and all seemed quite nonplussed. To add to other difficulties there were no signs of young Fred Oliver, who, as the deputy of Old Tom, had charge of the ropes and stakes, although he had distinct notice on Friday at what time the expedition was to leave London. This state of things cast a gloom on the travellers, many of whom had serious thoughts of returning to town. On persuasion, however, they made up their minds to 'see it out,' and as the train could not be stopped, all resumed their seats and sped on to Southend, hoping to find Caunt there, or, at any rate, to hear some tidings of him. On reaching this spot all at once made their way to the pier head, but not a word could be heard of the ex-Champion, or of the ropes and stakes. Butler at once went on board one boat (that reserved for first-class passengers), while Dan Dismore remained on the pier to supply tickets for the voyage.

The party now boarded the second-class boat, where Nat was found installed, waiting impatiently for the appearance of Caunt, of whom nothing could be heard; Dan Dismore also came on board this vessel.

It was now nearly twelve o'clock and all began anxiously to look for the half-hour, at which time the next train was due at Southend, by which it was, of course, expected that Ben would come. Half-past twelve, one o'clock arrived, the train had been in some time, but still there was no appearance of Ben on the pier. At length an emissary was sent ashore and he ascertained that Caunt and the ropes and stakes had been embarked on board an opposition tug, singularly enough called the 'Ben Bolt,' at Tilbury and that they were on the way to join the flotilla as quickly as possible. It was two o'clock or nearly so before the 'Ben Bolt' hove into sight, with the other Ben on board.

By a quarter-past two o'clock, everything being settled, the office was given and an experienced pilot conducted the flotilla, which now numbered four steamboats, besides innumerable small craft, to the proposed scene of action and the boats steamed away for the Standing Creek, on the Medway, where the party was landed, immediately opposite to the spot where Sayers and Aaron Jones had fought their battle. Against a strong ebb of course progress was very slow and it was past three before the first vessel arrived off the point.

The ropes and stakes were at once sent ashore and Fred Oliver with due diligence proceeded to erect the ring. Poor Old Tom was sadly missed and many expressions of regret were uttered at his continued ill health. The number of persons present was extremely large, but of Corinthians there was a lamentable absence, arising, no doubt, from the before-mentioned suspicions as to the men's intentions.

As soon as the arena was ready, the combatants, who were evidently all agog to be at it, tossed their caps into the ring, Nat being the first to uncover his canister, Ben being not two seconds behind him. Both looked hard and healthy, but their mugs bore distinct traces of their being veteran boxers. Ben, of course, looked the older man, his not handsome dial being as brown as mahogany and looked as hard as a nutmeg-grater. Nat's phiz was smoother, softer and of a lighter tint and there was a hue of health upon it that had not been seen there for many a day. They shook hands, but it was evident that the ceremony was against the grain.

At a quarter to four the seconds proceeded to knot the colours on the centre stake - a blue, with white spot, for Langham, orange with a blue border for Caunt.

As four o'clock was fast approaching, it was hinted that no time ought to be lost and the men at once proceeded to accomplish their toilets. Nat Langham was assisted by the Champion (Tom Sayers) and the accomplished Jack Macdonald - certainly the best second out - while Ben Caunt was waited upon (we cannot say picked up, for he never once was down throughout the fight) by Jack Gill, of Nottingham and Jemmy Shaw, who, between them, could never have carried him to his corner, had occasion required it, in the time allowed between the rounds, indeed they must have inevitably have carried him a limb at a time. How he could have been persuaded to select two such assistants it is hard to understand. Jack Gill could not have had much experience in his new vocation and Jemmy Shaw will excuse us for saying that, however staunch a friend and good fellow he had proved himself in other ways, his stature and proportions by no means qualified him as a porter to either Gog or Magog, should those gigantic worthies need to be picked up from a horizontal position.

The ring was soon pitched and the men entered.

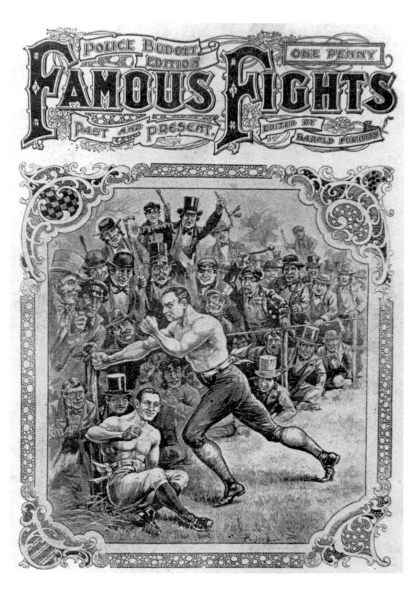

Ben Caunt and Nat Langham

THE FIGHT

Round 1:
On toeing the scratch the disparity between the men was of course extraordinary. Ben Caunt, barring his mug, was a study for a sculptor. His massive frame and powerful legs and arms - the former set off to best advantage by pink silk stockings and well made drawers - presented a sight worth going some distance to see; and as he stood over old Nat any one would have agreed with Jerry Noon, who declared that it was 'Chelsea Hospital to a sentry-box' in his favour. He smiled good-humouredly and had clearly made up his mind to win in a trot. Nat was, as usual, clear in skin and neatly made at all points. His shoulders and arms were well covered with muscle and for an encounter with a man of his own size he looked all that could be desired; but as to his being a match for Ben Caunt it seemed too absurd to be credited and few expected to see him perform with anything like effect. His attitude, as of yore, was perfection and his dangerous left was playing about close to his side all in readiness for one of his neat deliveries as Ben came in. Caunt stood just as he ever stood, very square on his pins, his brawny arms almost straight out before him, which he ever and anon moved backward and forward with all the deliberation of a couple of pendulums. He had come, however, not to spar, but to fight and after very little feinting he went up to Nat, who retreated towards the ropes and Ben at length lunged out left and right, just catching Nat with the former on the ribs and Nat was down laughing.

Round 2:
Both very quick to respond to "Time". Caunt walked after Nat and as he got close he sent out his left, but Nat, quick as lightning, shot out his left on the kisser, drawing first blood from Ben's upper lip and got down.

Round 3:
After a little dodging Nat feinted and then let fly his left straight on the jaw. Slight exchanges followed on the side of the wig block and Nat was again down out of harm's way.

Round 4:
No time cut to waste, Caunt went to his man and poked out his left, just catching Nat on the chin and Nat dropped.

Round 5:
Nat fiddled Ben to within distance and then popped his 'larboard daddle'[32] on Ben's jaw, a cracker; this led to heavy exchanges, Caunt getting on to Nat's forehead above the left peeper and receiving on the cheek; Nat fell.

Round 6:
After one or two passes the men got close and very slight exchanges took place, when Nat got down by a roll over.

Round 7:
Caunt stalked up to Nat, swung his mauleys slowly round and then dropped the left on Nat's left cheek, Nat nailing him prettily at the same time on the left eye; Nat down clumsily, Caunt carefully stepping over him.

Round 8:
Caunt again approached Nat and lunged out his left, Nat countering him quickly on the right peeper. Ben got home on the left cheek and Nat fell.

Round 9:
Nat dodged about for an opening and then got sharply home on the left cheek. Caunt returned very slightly on the side of the nut and Nat was down.

Round 10:
Both sparred a little for wind, but soon went to close quarters, when, after a very slight exchange on the forehead, Nat sought Mother Earth.

Round 11:
Similar to previous round with Caunt missing with both hands.

Round 12:
Nat, after a few passes, got within distance and shot out his left as straight as a dart on Ben's conk, inflicting an ugly cut on the bridge and drawing more claret. The blow had double force from the fact that Ben was coming in at the time. He, nevertheless, bored in and had Nat down at the ropes.

Round 13:
Nat again timed his man to perfection with his left on the proboscis and

---

[32] Right fist

slipped down from the force of the blow. He recovered himself, however and after a little sparring got sharply on Ben's potato-trap[33]. Ben retaliated, but not effectively, on Nat's cheek and Nat fell.

Round 14:
Nat feinted and dropped smartly on the snorer. He tried again, but missed and in getting away slipped down.

Round 15:
Langham missed his left and slight exchanges followed at the ropes, where Nat got down, Caunt again, in the most manly way, refraining from falling on him, as he might have done as he was going down.

Round 16:
Ben took the first move and got home, but not heavily, on Nat's jaw. They then sparred a bit and on getting close Caunt lunged out his one, two, on Nat's left cheek, but the blows appeared to have no steam in them. Nat popped a straight one on the left brow and dropped.

Round 17:
Slight exchanges, no damage and Ben bored his man down at the ropes.

Round 18:
Nat let fly his left, but Ben was too far off. Ben, however, went to him and slight exchanges took place, Nat on the mark and Caunt on the side of the head and Nat down.

Round 19:
After slight exchanges, Ben got home sharply on the back of Nat's brain pan and Nat fell.

Round 20:
No time lost. They walked up to one another and at once let fly, Caunt on Nat's forehead and Nat on the left brow. Nat down.

Round 21:
Good exchanges, but Nat straightest, getting another good one on Ben's conk and renewing the crimson distillation. Caunt touched Nat's forehead

---

[33] The mouth

and Nat down without a visible mark of punishment.

Round 22:
Caunt rushed at Nat, who being close to the ropes, slipped down. An appeal of "Foul" was made, but not by the umpires. The referee, however, sent Nat's umpire to him to caution him.

Round 23:
Nat fiddled and dodged until Caunt drew back his arm, when pop went the left on Ben's cheek. Exchanges followed, Nat getting on Ben's left peeper and Ben on the brow and Nat down.

Round 24:
Slight exchanges; Ben on the forehead and Nat down.

Round 25:
Nat missed his first delivery, but in a second effort caught Ben on the body, Caunt retaliating with a swinging round hit on the cranium and Nat down.

Round 26:
Sharp exchanges; Nat on the kisser and Ben on the side of the canister and Nat down, Ben as usual stepping over him, but asking him why he 'did not stand up and have a round.'

Round 27:
Ben went to his man and began business by lunging out both hands, but he missed and Nat popped his left on the whistler. Ben, however, returned on the cheek, just drawing claret and Nat down.

Round 28:
Ben again succeeded in reaching Nat's cheek with his right, drawing the ruby and Nat fell.

Rounds 29 and 30:
After trifling exchanges in these rounds Nat got down, much to the annoyance of Ben, who, however, preserved his good temper and merely remonstrated with his cunning opponent.

Round 31:
Nat dodged and popped his left sharply on the mazzard, received the merest

The parlour at The Coach and Horses

excuse for a blow and dropped.

Round 32:
In this round the exchanges were very slight, but Nat's were straightest. As usual, he was down.

Round 33:
Nat crept in, let go his left on Ben's lip, which he cut and Nat fell on his back from the force of his own blow.

Round 34:
Ben, whose warbler[34] was bleeding, rushed at Nat furiously and regularly bored him down.

Rounds 35 to 47:
To go into details of the next few rounds would be merely a repetition of what is already written. Nat feinted, dodged, timed his man with the greatest precision whenever he moved his arms and, although his blows did not seem very heavy, they still were always there, or thereabouts and poor old Ben's mug began to be all shapes. The manly fellow, however, never grumbled; he went straight up to be planted upon and although he occasionally got home a body blow or a round hit on the side of Nat's knowledge box, still he left no visible marks. Once or twice Jemmy Shaw claimed "Foul," on the ground that Nat fell without a blow; but Nat was cunning enough to keep just within the pale of the law. There was not one round in which he did not go down and Ben invariably walked to his corner. In the 43rd round Ben got the first knock-down blow on Nat's forehead.

Round 48:
Ben bustled in with desperation, but Nat met him full in the mouth and then on the snorter, with his left, drawing the crimson from each, Ben returned on the top of the forehead and Nat got down.

Round 49:
Nat crept in craftily and popped a little one on the snuffer-tray[35] and this led to a tremendous counter-hit, Caunt on the cheek and Nat on the jaw very

---

[34] The mouth
[35] The nose

heavily, drawing more ruby. Nat fell, his nut first reaching the ground and Ben staggered to his corner, evidently all abroad. By great exertions and a little extra time, his seconds got him up to the scratch. Nat, however, was not in a much better state. Both were severely shaken.

Round 50:
Nat on coming up, was evidently slow, but, to the surprise of every one, showed no mark of the hit in the last round, while Ben's kisser was considerable awry and he was scarcely himself. Now would have been Langham's time, but he had not strength to go in. After a short spar, Ben got on to Nat's jaw, staggering him; Nat returned sharply on the left eye and nozzle. After heavy exchanges on the body, Nat fell.

Round 51:
In this round Ben just missed Nat as he was falling and caught the stake very heavily with his left, which was thereby rendered useless, or nearly so.

Rounds 52 to 60:
There was nothing to call for particular notice. Nat pursued his defensive tactics and his pop for nothing when there was a chance. Still, however, old Ben kept swinging his dangerous limbs about and every now and then got heavily on Nat's body and left shoulder and occasionally on the top of his head. Nat fell every round, but often times he had to do it so quickly, owing to the close proximity of Ben, that he fell most awkwardly for himself and must have been shaken severely. He gradually got tired and Caunt, whose dial was much cut about, was evidently puzzled what to be at. At length, in the sixtieth round, after a little sparring and a slight exchange, they stood and looked at one another and rubbed their chests. Neither seemed disposed to begin and it was pretty clear that each had the same end in view - namely, to protract the battle until it was dark. Each, doubtless, felt that he was unable to finish that day and did not feel disposed to throw a chance away by going in and getting an unexpected finisher at close quarters.

There is nothing to describe after that. Darkness was setting in and although Caunt in his terrific lunges nearly succeeded in knocking Langham out, the latter was too quick. At length both seemed to have had enough of it and they stood for many minutes rubbing their chests and looking at each other and it was evident that they were waiting for darkness to make it a draw. Dan Dismore then went to Mr. Frank Dowling, editor of Bell's Life and had an earnest conversation with him, for he was referee. Dan then stepped into the ring and asked the men to shake hands. Ben said he was willing to do so if Nat was. The latter, after slight hesitation, extended his hand, which was shaken heartily and the men dressed.

After standing several minutes, Dan Dismore said it was a pity that men who had been such close friends should proceed any further with hostilities and suggested that it would be much better if they forgave and forgot their quarrel and shook hands. The Editor of Bell's Life agreed with Dan in his kindly opinion and he then took upon himself to go into the ring and suggest some arrangement and in doing so he said he would gladly give £5 out of his own pocket to see them bury their animosity there and then and draw their stakes. Caunt said he was willing if Nat was and after a little consideration Nat held out his mauley, which was cordially shaken by Ben and then Langham went with Caunt into the corner of the latter, where he shook hands with Ben Butler and also with Caunt's son. Dan Dismore now left the ring and on the referee asking him what had been done, Dan said, "It is all over; it's settled." The referee inquired whether they intended drawing altogether and Dan said again, "It's all done with; there will be nothing more done in it;" or words to that effect. The referee at once, on hearing this, expressed his pleasure at so amicable an arrangement and on the men quitting the arena he also left the ring side, his office of course ceasing and on the faith of Dan's statement he at once gave up what bets he held.

After being some time on board the boat, however, he was somewhat staggered at being accosted by one of Nat's Corinthian patrons and Jack Macdonald, who told him that Nat was quite astonished when they had mentioned to him that a draw had been agreed to and had declared that such a thing never entered his head. He thought Dismore merely wished them to draw for the time being and that the referee would name another day in the same week to fight again. The referee replied that his impression certainly was that an arrangement had been made to draw stakes, or he should not have vacated his post and this application on Nat's behalf took him so much by surprise that he did not know how his position was affected. It was a case that had never occurred before and he must think it over. Nat's backer said he also was impressed at the time with the notion that everything was arranged and had left the ring side with that belief, but still he thought the referee had the power to name another day, as Nat had been no party to any final arrangement.

At the railway station, on the arrival of the boats, the referee called both the men together and asked them in the presence of each other what they had understood on leaving the ring. Caunt said he understood they were friends again and were to draw their money, while Nat repeated the statement that had been conveyed to the referee by Jack Macdonald. Caunt seemed quite taken aback, as did also his friends. Dan Dismore now came up and repeated the statement that he had previously made, to the effect that he had recommended the men to shake hands and be friends and that he had certainly said he would give £5 out of his own pocket to see the matter settled. They had shaken hands at his recommendation and at the time it certainly had been his impression that they would not fight again. He declined, however, to take upon himself the responsibility of saying that either man had actually said anything about drawing stakes. The referee was now completely nonplussed and said, at that time and in such a crowd, he could not undertake to give an opinion either way. He then suggested that the men and their friends should meet at the Stakeholder's office the following day to discuss the matter, when all were calm and had had time to think over the affair.

Owing to the low state of the tide when the fight was over and the narrowness of the causeway to the boats, a great deal of time was lost in embarkation and not a few of the travellers obtained mud baths at much less price than such a luxury would have cost in Germany. The consequence of the delay was that the 8 o'clock train was missed and there being no other until 9.30, the travellers, weary, muddy and wet, but tolerably well satisfied with their entertainment, did not reach the Metropolis until twelve o'clock.

The following morning the referee took the opportunity of laying the case before a Corinthian patron of the art, who, although no longer a frequenter of the ring side, was for many years one of the staunchest attendants. That gentleman, after thinking the matter over for a few minutes, said he was of the opinion there could be no doubt as to the course of the referee. There had been, he said, no appeal to him to stop the fight - there was no reason for his interference, as he could see both men perfectly and he had stated there was sufficient daylight for eight or ten more rounds. The men had shaken hands in the ring and, putting Dismore and his statement out of the question as unnecessary adjuncts to the case, he was of the opinion that the men, by voluntarily quitting the ring without any appeal being made by themselves or their umpires, had clearly taken the whole affair out of the referee's hands and altogether deprived him of any power in the matter.

At the appointed hour both men and their friends were in attendance - Nat all but unscathed, while Ben had an ugly cut on his nose and his left peeper was partially closed. He had also other severe marks of punishment on various parts of his dial and his hands were much puffed. Both men made their statements. Caunt repeated that he fully believed Nat had agreed to draw stakes when he shook hands with him and his uncle, or he should never have consented to leave off fighting, as there was still daylight for ten or a dozen rounds. He was then warm and felt confident he could have won. He was as strong as ever on his legs and was convinced that Nat had done all he knew. Langham, in reply, denied that this was the case. He understood that Dismore only proposed a postponement until another day, as it was not likely they could finish that evening. He shook hands with Caunt and his uncle because he did not think he ought to leave the ring without performing that ceremony. Dan Dismore repeated the statement he had already made, adding that he certainly was not authorised to say they had agreed to draw their money, whatever his own impression might have been. He was of opinion then that it would have been a proper course and that opinion he still entertained; and he would willingly give £5 or £10 out of his own pocket to see them shake hands and make up their differences. Tom Sayers, who was also present, said he had left the ring with the idea that his principal had agreed to draw the money and he had no idea until some time afterwards that Nat had contemplated a renewal of hostilities.

The referee, after hearing both sides, said that he had thought the matter over very carefully and come to a conclusion in his own mind, before consulting the gentleman above referred to and he was glad to find that conclusion coincided with the opinion of his adviser. The men had taken the matter quite out of his hands. They had made an arrangement between themselves, had shaken hands and left the ring without asking his opinion, or appealing to him in any way. Although he stood close to the ropes and stakes at the time they were shaking hands, what other conclusion could he arrive at than that they had amicably settled their differences? That a misunderstanding had arisen as to future arrangements was to be regretted, but he had no power whatever to name another day. If his advice were asked it would be that they should shake hands, but if they did not choose to do this, they must agree upon another day and place between themselves. Nat at once proposed fighting again on Saturday, to which Caunt objected.

He said he was now stiff and his hands were injured and required time to get round. He believed a bone in one of his fingers was broken. As he had before said, he could have finished it the same night, but he should decline agreeing to fight again at present. Nat then asked what he proposed, to which Ben said he proposed that on the next occasion Nat should stand up and fight like a man. He could not fight a man who was always on the ground. A good deal of angry discussion followed, Ben Butler again going beyond the bounds of decorum, while Caunt remained perfectly quiet. Nat was, of course, incensed at being balked of his rights, as he considered them, but still there was no prospect of an arrangement. At length Nat asked Caunt to give him some portion of the stakes, as an inducement to draw a proposition indignantly scouted by Caunt. This was the last offer. The men were then informed that the referee had given his decision, that he could not interfere and it remained for them to agree between themselves upon a time and place.

Unartistic as he was, however, no one will deny that Caunt upheld the character he has invariably borne of a manly upright boxer, disdaining to avail himself of repeated opportunities, which many persons would unscrupulously have adopted, of falling on an opponent when he dropped in the not very manly manner that Nat, on many occasions, certainly did. From first to last Ben never lost his temper. He received all Nat's props with the greatest sang froid[36], smiling upon him and sometimes shaking his head at him for his shiftiness. As to Caunt's game, there never was and never can be, a question. He was punished most severely and yet he never once flinched or showed signs of not liking it. The only remark he condescended to make from time to time in his corner was that Nat had done all he could and that he must be getting weak. He did not wish to win by a foul and on several occasions when his seconds desired to appeal he said he would rather try to win on his merits. The fight lasted one hour and twenty-nine minutes.

The floodgates of newspaper letter writing were opened by this undecided encounter. It is needless to say that the controversy ended in much ink shedding and a draw of the £400 staked, leaving the debateable question of 'getting down to finish the round' much where it previously and subsequently stood.

---

[36] Imperturbability especially under strain

On the way home, though, Langham wanted to say that he had had no intention of finishing the battle, that he only considered it an adjournment and that the referee must name another day in the same week. This Mr. Dowling refused to do, so there was a tremendous row and they were as bad friends as ever, but after a wordy warfare in the sporting papers they met and drew the stakes, shaking hands and making it up, remaining friends until Caunt's death, in 1861.

From this period Caunt may be said to have finally retired from the Prize Ring, though he still kept his house, the Coach and Horses, in St Martin's Lane where the parlour was a general resort of aspirants for pugilistic honours and their patrons. Ben busied himself in bringing forward and occasionally backing or finding backers for fighters who included his brother Bob. He would also entertain the visitors to his inn with his party trick of squeezing a pint pewter pot completely flat using only the fingers of one hand.

The Coach and Horses became a far more unruly place as can be seen from the following which appeared in The Times Newspaper on October 2nd 1858:

Marlborough Street - Mr Benjamin Caunt was summoned before Mr Bingham for having his public house the Coach and Horses, St Martin's Lane, open at irregular hours and permitting disorderly conduct therein, on the 27th.

Police constable F125 said he heard a great noise in the defendant's house at 20 minutes past 1 o'clock a.m. and in the company of another policeman knocked several times at the door. For some time admission was refused, the noise continuing all the time. About five minutes he was waiting, during which he heard a voice call out, "Stand clear; let them have fair play!" Five minutes after the door was opened by Mrs Caunt. He told her it was wrong to have persons in the house at that time; there were two men stripped in front of the bar and he told her it was very wrong to allow a fight there at that hour in the morning. Mrs Caunt told him to go away about his business and at the same time pushed the door to and would not let him enter.

By Mr Edward Lewis, who appeared for the defendant.
The defendant was not present; he was sure of the time, for he looked at his watch, also at the house clock. Mrs Caunt did not say her husband was ill, but she did say he was in bed; nor did she promise to clear the house as quick as

she could. She said she should not. She did not explain that the two men had merely been quarrelling over their beer. One of the two men was so badly injured in the fight as to be obliged to go to the hospital to have his arm dressed.

Mr Lewis submitted that, as a sporting house, there was none in London better conducted than that of the defendant, which he had been the landlord of for 16 years, during which time he had only been twice summoned.

Mr Bingham said, the complaint, as shown by the evidence, was more against the defendant's wife than himself. Ladies were apt to be impetuous and were not always so discreet in their answers as the other sex. The defendant, was no doubt, a man of judgement, but he must manage to close his house at the proper hour and rule his customers; to do the latter he was certainly big enough. (A laugh).

The summons must be dismissed on payment of the costs.

Caunt's wife Martha died on June 1st 1859 and the inn continued to deteriorate until the licence was eventually lost.

In his later years Caunt was also well known as no mean performer with racing pigeons, on the various club grounds near the Metropolis and in Hertfordshire. Having caught a severe cold in a long day's match 'at the doves,' in the early part of 1860, it settled on his lungs and coupled with late hours and the free living inseparable from his calling as a publican, gave the powerful pugilist his final knock-down blow on the tenth day of September, 1861.

The following appeared in The Times Newspaper on 11th September 1861:

Yesterday morning, at 4 o'clock, Mr. Benjamin Caunt, the proprietor of the Coach and Horses Tavern, St. Martin's Lane, expired somewhat suddenly at his residence. The deceased, familiarly known as Ben Caunt, had long been a leading member of the Prize Ring and held for some years the championship, which he succeeded in gaining after many hard fought battles. All day yesterday Caunt was in his business as usual, but showed some signs of indisposition. He retired to rest at his usual hour last night and this morning he was found dead in bed, without having apparently experienced very much suffering. During the last year or two Caunt has been very much affected in his mind by the loss of his licence, of which the magistrates deprived him on account of information laid against him by his neighbours of the nuisance occasioned about his house by large crowds of sporting men who took an interest in the then pending prize-fights - particularly in that between Heenan and Sayers for the championship, which Caunt himself had just resigned. When his body was discovered at 4 o'clock this morning, the time at which he was usually called, medical aid was immediately resorted to; but it was ascertained that death must have taken place some time previously - probably an hour or two. Information of Caunt's decease has been forwarded to Mr. Langham, the deputy-coroner for Middlesex, who will no doubt fix a time for an inquest in the course of the day.

Caunt was buried in St Mary Magdalene parish church in Hucknall market place and it was reported that in the latter part of the nineteenth century more people visited the grave of Ben Caunt than visited the tomb of poet Lord Byron who is buried at the same church.

It is a very different matter these days though, with Ben Caunt almost a forgotten man.

The death mask of Ben Caunt

Chapter 11

TODAY

(2003)

1. The Coach and Horses Inn

Currently called The Salisbury it is described by CAMRA as follows:

One of the great turn-of-the-nineteenth-century palace pubs of London. It is part of a six-storey red-brick block built about 1899 and which incorporates a much older pub site. This site was leased from the Marquis of Salisbury in 1892 - hence the present name. Previously the pub had been variously known as the Coach & Horses and the Ben Caunt's Head. The exterior with its etched and polished glass and carved woodwork to the window frames gives some idea of what to expect inside - a splendid example of pub fitting as practised at the height of the boom around 1900. First of all the planning. The pub is remarkable for retaining one of its timber and glass screens and which marks off a small bar on the St Martin's Court side of the pub. There would have been other such screens originally creating a cluster of bars round the servery in typical London fashion (go to the Prince Alfred, Maida

Vale to see the best surviving example). It is not hard to work out where they would have been. You will note, for example, the way the counter top changes from wood to white marble and clearly this denotes what would have been separate areas within the pub. The abundance of etched and polished glass creates a glittering atmosphere: note that the etching on the large mirrors on the long wall and in the room at the rear of the pub is modern (it dates from some time in the last third of the twentieth century). The owners Scottish & Newcastle sensitively restored the pub in 1999. The work amounted to no more than a thorough cleaning of the inside and outside and reupholstering of the seats and is thus a model of how historic pub fabrics should be treated - in the old maxim of conservationists, 'do what is necessary but as little as possible'. Grade II listed.

1. <u>Ben Caunt's Grave</u>

The iron railings surrounding the grave had been removed many years ago to help the war effort (metal was in great demand and items such as railings were removed up and down the country) and the grave and monument were allowed to fall into a state of disrepair with the soft sandstone headstone (five feet high and two feet square) deteriorating badly it meant that the slate inscriptions on three sides had fallen to the ground.

Fortunately in the 1980's, Hucknall residents Eileen West, a grandaughter of Caunt's daughter Margaret, her husband Derek and a friend Mr Danny Mills have done a first class job of restoring the grave.

The inscriptions read:

Panel 1: Ben Caunt, Champion of England, 1841-1845

Panel 2: A poem by Margaret in memory of her parents

Panel 3 records the death of Benjamin Caunt, aged 46, on September 10th 1861 and his wife Martha, aged 42, on June 1st, 1859.

Panel 4: Martha Caunt, aged 8 and Cornelius, aged 6, beloved children of Benjamin and Martha Caunt, natives of this town, whose residence in St. Martin's Lane, London, accidentally taking fire early in the morning of 16th June 1851, they unhappily perished.

APPENDIX 1

Ben Caunt's record in the Prize Ring

As a youngster Ben fought a number of minor and unrecorded fights before embarking on his Prize Ring career. These included a relative, Richard Butler at Wighay Field in Hucknall and George Graham of Lincolnshire both of which he won.

1835   July 21st Bendigo, Lost, 22 rounds, £25, Nottingham

1837   Aug 17th William Butler, Won, 14 rounds, £20, Stoneyford Notts

1837   Nov 4th Bill Boneford, Won, 6 rounds, £25, Sunrise Hill Nottingham

1838   Apr 3rd Bendigo, Won, 75 rounds, £100, Skipworth Common

1840   Oct 27th Bill Brassey, Won, 101 rounds, £100, Six Mile Bottom

1841   Feb 2nd Nick Ward, Lost, 7 rounds, £100, Crookham Common

1841   May 11th Nick Ward, Won, 35 rounds, £100, Long Marsden

1845   Sep 9th Bendigo, Lost, 93 rounds, £200, Stoney Stratford

1857   Sep 23rd Nat Langham, Drew, 60 rounds, £200, London

APPENDIX II

Broughton's Rules of 1743 which would govern prize-fighting for almost a century.

I. That a square of a yard be chalked in the middle of the stage; and on every fresh set-to after a fall, or being parted from the rails, each second is to bring his man to the side of the square and place him opposite to the other and till they are fairly set-to at the lines, it shall not be lawful for one to strike at the other.

II. That, in order to prevent any disputes, the time a man lies after a fall, if the second does not bring his man to the side of the square, within the space of half a minute, he shall be deemed a beaten man.

III. That in every main battle, no person whatever shall be upon the stage, except the principals and their seconds; the same rule to be observed in bye-battles, except that in the latter, Mr. Broughton is allowed to be upon the stage to keep decorum and to assist gentlemen in getting in their places, provided always he does not interfere in the battle; and whoever pretends to infringe these rules to be turned immediately out of the house. Everybody is to quit the stage as soon as the champions are stripped, before the set-to.

IV. That no champion be deemed beaten, unless he fails coming up to the line in the limited time, or that his own second declares him beaten. No second is to be allowed to ask his man's adversary any questions, or advise him to give out.

V. That in bye-battles, the winning man to have two-thirds of the money given, which shall be publicly divided upon the stage, notwithstanding any private agreements to the contrary.

VI. That to prevent disputes, in every main battle the principals shall, on coming on the stage, choose from among the gentlemen present two umpires, who shall absolutely decide all disputes that may arise about the battle; and if the two umpires cannot agree, the said umpires to choose a third, who is to determine it.

VII. That no person is to hit his adversary when he is down, seize him by the ham, the breeches, or any part below the waist: a man on his knees to be reckoned down.

As agreed by Several Gentlemen at Broughton's Amphitheatre, Tottenham Court Road, August 16, 1743.

APPENDIX III

London Prize Ring Rules, 1838
(Revised 1853)

1. The ring shall be made on the turf and shall be four and twenty feet square, formed of eight stakes and ropes, the latter extending lines, the uppermost line being four feet from the ground and the lower two feet from the ground. In the centre of the ring a mark to be formed to be termed a scratch.

2. Each man shall be attended to the ring by two seconds and a bottle-holder. The combatants, on shaking hands, shall retire until the seconds have tossed for choice of positions, which adjusted, the winner shall choose at his corner, according to the state of the wind or sun and conduct his man thereto, the loser taking the opposite diagonal corner.

3. Each man shall be provided with a handkerchief of a colour suitable to his own fancy and the seconds shall entwine these handkerchiefs at the upper end of one of the centre stakes. These handkerchiefs shall be called 'colours' and the winner of the battle, at its conclusion, shall be entitled to their possession as the trophy of victory.

4. The two umpires shall be chosen by the seconds or backers to watch the progress of the battle and take exception to any breach of the rules hereinafter stated. A referee shall be chosen by the umpires unless otherwise agreed upon, to whom all disputes shall be referred; and the decision of this referee, whatever it may be, shall be final and strictly binding on all parties, whether as to the matter in dispute or the issue of the battle. The referee shall be provided with a watch for the purpose of calling time, the calling of that referee only to be attended to and no other person whatever shall interfere in calling time. The referee shall withhold all opinion till appealed to by the umpires and the umpires strictly abide by his decision without dispute.

5. On the men being stripped it shall be the duty of the seconds to examine their drawers and if any objection arises as to the insertion of improper substances therein, they shall appeal to their umpires, who,

with the concurrence of the referee, shall direct what alterations shall be made.

6. The spikes in the fighting boots shall be confined to three in number, which shall not exceed three-eighths of an inch from the sole of the boot and shall not be less than one-eighth of an inch broad at the point; two to be placed in the broadest part of the sole and one in the heel; and in the event of a man wearing any other spikes, either in toes or elsewhere, he shall be compelled either to remove them, or provide other boots properly spiked, the penalty for refusal to be a loss of the stakes.

7. Both men being ready, each shall be conducted to that side of the scratch next his corner previously chosen; and, the seconds on the one side and the men on the other, having shaken hands, the former shall immediately leave the ring and there remain until the round be finished, on no pretence whatever approaching their principals during the round without permission from the referee, the penalty to be the loss of the battle to the offending parties.

8. At the conclusion of the round when one or both of the men shall be down, the seconds shall step into the ring and carry or conduct their principal to his corner, there affording him the necessary assistance and no person whatever be permitted to interfere in this duty.

9. On the expiration of thirty seconds the referee appointed shall cry 'Time,' upon which each man shall rise from the knee of his second and walk to his own side of the scratch unaided; the seconds immediately leaving the ring. The penalty for either of them remaining eight seconds after the call of time to be the loss of the battle to his principal; and either man failing to be at the scratch within eight seconds shall be deemed to have lost the battle.

10. On no consideration whatever shall any person except the seconds and the referee be permitted to enter the ring during the battle, nor till it shall have been concluded; and in the event of such unfair practice, or the ropes or stakes being removed or disturbed, it shall be in the power of the referee to award the victory to the man who, in his honest opinion, shall have the best of the contest.

11. The seconds shall not interfere, advise, or direct the adversary of their principal and shall refrain from all offensive and irritating expressions, in all respects conducting themselves with order and decorum and confine themselves to the diligent and careful discharge of their duties to their principals.

12. In picking up their men, should the seconds wilfully injure the antagonist of their principal, the latter shall be deemed to have forfeited the battle on the decision of the referee.

13. It shall be a fair stand-up fight and if either man shall wilfully throw himself down without receiving a blow, whether blows shall have been previously exchanged or not, he shall be deemed to have lost the battle; but this rule shall not apply to a man who in a close slip down from the grasp of his opponent to avoid punishment, or from obvious accident or weakness.

14. Butting with the head shall be deemed a foul and the party resorting to this practice shall be deemed to have lost the battle.

15. A blow struck when a man is thrown or down shall be deemed foul. A man with one knee and one hand on the ground, or with both knees on the ground shall be deemed down and a blow given in either of the positions shall be considered foul, providing always that, when in such position, the man so down shall not himself strike, or attempt to strike.

16. A blow struck below the waistband and in a close, seizing an antagonist below or otherwise shall be deemed foul.

17. All attempts to inflict injury by gouging or tearing flesh with the fingers or nails and biting shall be deemed foul.

18. Kicking or deliberately falling on an antagonist with knees or otherwise, when down, shall be deemed foul.

19. All bets shall be paid as the battle money after the fight is awarded.

20. The referee and umpires shall take their positions in front of the centre stake outside the ropes,

21. Due notice shall be given by the stakeholder of the day and place where the battle money is to be given up and be exonerated from all responsibility upon obeying the direction of the referee; all parties to be strictly bound by these rules and in future all articles of agreement for a contest be entered into with a strict and willing adherence to the letter and spirit of these rules.

22. In the event of magisterial or other interference, or in the case of darkness coming on, the referee (or stakeholder in case no referee has been chosen) shall have the power to name the time and place for the next meeting, if possible, on the same day, or as soon after as may be. In naming the second or third place, the nearest spot shall be selected to the original place of fighting where there is a chance of its being fought out.

23. Should the fight not be decided on the day, all bets shall be drawn, unless the fight shall be resumed the same week, between Sunday and Sunday, in which case the referee's duties shall continue and the bets shall stand and be decided by the event. The battle money shall remain in the hands of the stakeholder until fairly won or lost by a fight, unless a draw be mutually agreed upon, or, in case of a postponement, one of the principals shall be absent, when the man in the ring shall be awarded the stakes.

24. Any pugilist voluntarily quitting the ring previous to the deliberate judgment of the referee being obtained shall be deemed to have lost the fight.

25. On an objection being made by the seconds or umpires the men shall retire to their corners and there remain until the decision of the appointed authorities shall be obtained; if pronounced "Foul" the battle shall be at an end, but if "Fair" time shall be called by the party appointed and the men absent from the scratch eight seconds after shall be deemed to have lost the fight. The decision in all cases is to be given promptly and irrevocably, for which purpose the umpires and the referee should be invariably close together.

26. If a man leaves the ring, either to escape punishment or for any other purpose without the permission of the referee, unless he is involuntarily forced out, he shall forfeit the battle.

27. The use of hard substances, such as stones or sticks, or of resin in the hand during the battle, shall be deemed foul and on the requisition of the seconds of either man, the accused shall open his hands for the examination of the referee.

28. Hugging on the ropes shall be deemed foul. A man held by the neck against the stakes or upon or against the ropes, shall be considered down and all interference with him in that position shall be deemed foul. If a man in any way makes use of the ropes or stakes to aid him in squeezing his adversary, he shall be deemed the loser of the battle and if a man in close reaches the ground with his knee, his adversary shall immediately loose him or lose the battle.

29. All glove or room fights to be as nearly possible in conformity with the foregoing rules.

APPENDIX IV

Transcript of the Will of Benjamin Caunt

1853

This is the last Will and Testament of me, Benjamin Caunt of St Martin's Lane in the Parish of St Martin in the Fields in the County of Middlesex, Publican,

I appoint John Nathan Bainbridge of St Martin's Lane aforesaid, Doctor of Medicine and Thomas Woolley Marshall of St Martin's Lane aforesaid, Draper, to be Trustees and Executors of this my Will and I appoint my dear wife Martha Caunt and after her death the said John Nathan Bainbridge and Thomas Woolley Marshall and the survivors and survivor of them, to be Guardians and Guardian of my infant Children,

I give and bequeath unto my said wife Martha Caunt and her assigns the sum of one hundred Pounds British Sterling and also all my Stock in trade, furniture, plate, linen, china, wearing apparel, wines, liquers [sic] and all other my Chattels and effects except trade fixtures, which shall at the time of my decease be in or about my dwelling house or premises in which I may then reside or carry on business, for her and their own absolute use and benefit,

I give and bequeath the dwelling house and premises in which I may carry on my said business of a Publican at the time of my decease unto my said wife for and during her natural life, provided she shall continue to pay all rent ["..." interlined] and outgoings thenceforth during her life to become due thereon and shall fulfil all and every the covenants, conditions and agreements contained in any then existing Lease, under which the same may be held at the time of my decease, but not otherwise and, subject thereto, I give and devise all the messuages, lands, hereditaments and real estate wheresoever situate and of what nature or tenure soever of or to which I am or at the time of my death shall be seized or entitled, either at Law or in Equity, or of which I have, or at the time of my death shall have, power to dispose by this my Will, unto and to the use of the said John Nathan Bainbridge and Thomas Woolley Marshall, their heirs, executors, administrators and assigns respectively, according to the nature and tenure thereof, respectively upon trust that they the said John Nathan Bainbridge and Thomas Woolley Marshall, or the survivor of them, or the heirs, executors or administrators respectively of such survivor shall, as soon as conveniently may be after my death, absolutely sell and dispose of the said messuages, lands and hereditaments and real estate either entirely and altogether or in parcels and either by public auction or by private contract, with power to buy in and to rescind any contract for sale of the said premises or any part thereof and to resell [sic] the same without being answerable for any loss which may happen thereby and also with power to insert any special or other stipulation in any contract for, or conditions of sale, either as to title or evidence of title or otherwise and with power to execute, make and do all such Conveyances, Surrenders, assurances and things for effectuating any such sale as aforesaid as may be necessary or expedient,

I give and bequeath all the money, securities for money, goods, Chattels, credits and personal Estate of or to which I am or at my death shall be possessed or entitled either at Law or in equity, or of which I have or at my death shall have power to dispose by Will, except Chattels ... included in the devise of real Estate hereinbefore contained and except what else I otherwise dispose of by this my Will, or any codicil thereto, unto the said John Nathan Bainbridge and Thomas Woolley Marshall, their executors, administrators and assigns, upon trust that they the said John Nathan Bainbridge and Thomas Woolley Marshall, or the survivor of them, or the executors or administrators of such survivor, shall as soon as conveniently may be after my death call in, sell and convert into money such parts thereof as shall not consist of money,

And I hereby declare that the said John Nathan Bainbridge and Thomas Woolley Marshall and the survivor of them and the heirs, executors and administrators respectively of such survivor shall by and out of the monies to arise from the sale of the said real estate hereinbefore devised in trust for sale and from the calling in sale and conversion into money of such parts of the said personal estate hereinbefore bequeathed as shall not consist of money and by and out of the ready money of which I shall be possessed at my death, except such part thereof as I have hereinbefore given to my said wife, pay my funeral and testamentary expences [sic] and costs and the Legacies bequeathed by any codicil to this my Will and shall invest the residue of the same monies in the names or name of them the said John Nathan Bainbridge and Thomas Woolley Marshall, or the survivor of them or the executors or administrators of such survivor, in or upon any of the Parliamentary Stocks or public Funds of Great Britain, or at interest upon Government securities, or on Mortgage of freehold ["or" omitted] Copyhold Estates or Leasehold Estates having at the least sixty years to run, or upon any other real Securities in

England or Wales, but not in Ireland and that they or he shall have power from time to time or at any time to alter, vary or transpose such Stocks, funds or securities into or for others of the same or a like nature at their or his discretion,

And do and shall stand and be possessed of and interested in all the said trust monies and the stocks, funds and securities in or upon which the same shall be laid out or invested and the interest, dividends and annual produce thereof, upon and for the trusts intents and purposes and with, under and subject to the powers, provisees? and declarations hereinafter expressed, declared and contained of and concerning the same, that is to say, upon trust that the said John Nathan Bainbridge and Thomas Woolley Marshall and the survivor of them and the executors and administrators of such survivor, shall pay the interest, dividends and annual produce thereof to, or permit the same to be received by, my said wife Martha Caunt during her life for her own sole and separate use and free from the control, debts or engagements of any future husband with whom she may intermarry,

And I declare that her receipt alone shall be a sufficient discharge from time to time for the same and that she shall not have any power to alienate, charge, incumber or anticipate the same,

And after her decease my said trustees shall stand and be possessed of the said trust monies, stocks, funds and securities and the interest, dividends and annual produce thereof, In trust for my children Benjamin Butler Caunt and Margaret Butler Caunt and all and every other such Child or children of mine then living and such issue then living of any Child or Children then deceased, as being a Male or Males, shall either before or after the death of my said wife attain the age of twenty one years, or being a female or females shall either before or after the same period attain that age or marry, as tenants in common in a course of distribution according to the stocks and not to the number of individual objects and so that the issue of deceased children may take by way of substitution the share or respective shares only that the parent or respective parents would if living having taken [sic],

And as to the share or shares of any Child or Children dying without attaining a vested interest or vested interests and without leaving issue living to attain such interest or interests, the same share and shares shall be held upon the trusts herein contained concerning the other share or shares,

And as to the share or shares of any Grandchild or Grandchildren dying without attaining a vested interest or vested interests, such last mentioned share or shares shall be held upon the trusts herein contained concerning the other share or shares of the same family of Grandchildren, provided always and I declare my Will to be, that it shall be lawful for the said John Nathan Bainbridge and Thomas Woolley Marshall and the survivor of them and the executors and administrators of such survivor, at any time or times after the decease of my said Wife, or in her lifetime with her consent in writing, to pay or apply any part or parts not exceeding one moiety of the portion or portions to which any child or children or grandchild or grandchildren of mine shall or may for the time being be presumptively entitled under any of the trusts hereinbefore declared of or in the said trust, monies, stocks, funds and securities for and towards the advancement or preferment in the world or benefit of such child or children or Grandchild or Grandchildren respectively, in such manner as to the said trustees or trustee, for the time being, shall seem expedient.

And I hereby further declare my Will to be that after the decease of my said wife the said John [badly written] Nathan Bainbridge and Thomas Woolley Marshall and the survivor of them and the executors and administrators of such survivor shall pay and apply the whole, or such part as they the said trustees or trustee for the time being shall think fit, of the interest, dividends and annual produce of the portion or portions to which any child or children or Grandchild or Grandchildren of mine shall for the time being be entitled in expectancy under any of the trusts hereinbefore declared for or towards his, her or their maintenance or education until his, her or their said ["then" interlined] expectant portion shall become vested and payable and that the said trustees or trustee for the time being may either themselves or himself so pay or apply the same, or my pay the same to the Guardian or Guardians of such Child or Children, Grandchild or Grandchildren for the purpose aforesaid without seeing to the application thereof.

Provided always and I hereby authorize my said Trustees to pay and apply the whole or such part of the dividends, interest and income of my said estate and effects for the maintenance of such child, Grandchild, children or Grandchildren [sic] in such parts, shares and proportions irrespective of their said expectant share or shares, or to accumulate the same as my said trustees shall think fit.

Provided always and I hereby further declare that it shall be lawful for the said John Nathan Bainbridge and Thomas Woolley Marshall and the survivor of them and the executors and administrators of such survivor at any time or times, with the consent in writing of my said Wife during her life and after her death at the sole discretion of the said trustees or trustee for the time being, to dispose of, call in and convert into money the whole or any part of the said trust monies, stocks, funds and securities and to lay out and invest the money arising therefrom, or any part thereof, in the purchase of any freehold, copyhold or customary Messuages, lands or hereditaments in England or Wales for any estate of inheritance, or any leasehold Messuages, lands or hereditaments in England or Wales for any term of years whereof not less than sixty years shall be to come and unexpired at the time of such purchase, to be conveyed, surrendered or assigned to them the said John Nathan Bainbridge and Thomas Woolley Marshall, or the survivor of them and their or his heirs, executors, administrators and assigns, according to the nature of the estate or interest therein, upon trust nevertheless that the said John Nathan Bainbridge and Thomas Woolley Marshall, or the survivor of them, or the heirs, executors and administrators of such survivor, do and shall with such consent or at such direction as last aforesaid, absolutely sell and dispose of the said Messuages, lands and tenements which shall have been so purchased as aforesaid, either entirely and altogether or in parcels and either by Public Auction or private contract for such price or prices and upon such conditions and with such stipulations as to title or evidence of title or otherwise and in such manner in every respect as the said John Nathan Bainbridge and Thomas Woolley Marshall, or the survivor of them, or the heirs, executors and administrators of such survivor shall think fit with full power to buy in the said premises or any part thereof at any Sale or Sales by public Auction and to rescind, abandon or vary any contract for Sale and to resell the premises which shall be so bought in or the contract for the sale of which shall be ["so" interlined] rescinded or abandoned as aforesaid, without being answerable for any loss which may happen thereby respectively.

And ["... and" interlined] shall stand and be possessed of and interested in and apply the money arising from any such sale, after payment of the costs, charges and expences attending the same, upon and for such and the same trusts intents and purposes and with, under and subject to such and the same powers, provisees? and declarations, including the said power of purchasing freehold, copyhold and leasehold hereditaments as the money so raised and laid out in the purchase of such Messuages, lands or hereditaments was subject to before such purchase was made, or would have been then subject to if the same had not been out therein [sic].

And I do hereby declare that the said John Nathan Bainbridge and Thomas Woolley Marshall and the survivor of them and the executors and administrators of such survivor, shall in every case have the most full and entire discretion as to the exercise or non exercise of the said power lastly hereinbefore contained of purchasing Lands or other property and the choice of the property which may be so purchased, both with respect to the position and nature thereof and the title thereto, but so that such consent as aforesaid in the cases hereinbefore mentioned be obtained.

Provided always and I hereby declare that it shall be lawful for the said John Nathan Bainbridge and Thomas Woolley Marshall and the survivor of them and the heirs, executors and administrators of such survivor, in the meantime and until all the said hereditaments and premises hereinbefore mentioned devised in trust for sale and the said hereditaments and premises which shall or may be purchased under the power hereinbefore contained, shall be sold as aforesaid to devise or lease all or any part of the same hereditaments and premises for any term or terms of years not exceeding twenty one years, to take effect in possession so as there be reserved the best yearly rent or rents that can be reasonably gotten [sic], without taking anything in the nature of a fine, premium or foregift and so as there be contained in every such devise or Lease a condition of reentry for nonpayment of the rent or rents thereby reserved and so as the lessee or lessees do execute a Counterpart thereof and be not thereby made dispunishable [sic] for waste.

And I hereby further declare that the said John Nathan Bainbridge and Thomas Woolley Marshall and the survivor of them and the heirs, executors or administrators respectively of such survivor, shall in the meantime and until the same hereditaments and premises respectively shall be so sold as aforesaid, pay or apply the rents and profits thereof, or of so much thereof as for the time being shall remain unsold, after payment thereout of all rates, taxes, payments for assurance against loss by fire, costs of repairs and other outgoings which any tenant or other person shall not be liable to pay to the person or persons for the purposes and in the manner to whom and for and in which the interest, dividends and annual produce of the monies to arise from such sale, or of the stocks, funds and securities in or upon which the same monies are hereinbefore directed to be invested would be payable or applicable under the trusts herein contained if the sale and investment as aforesaid were then actually made, it being my intent and meaning that the hereditaments and premises which shall be purchased under the power hereinbefore contained, as well as the hereditaments and premises hereinbefore devised in trust for sale, shall be considered as money and be subject to the same trusts in all respects as the money to arise from the sale thereof would under the provisions herein contained be subject to if the same were actually sold,

Provided always and I declare my Will to be, that it shall be lawful for the said John Nathan Bainbridge and Thomas Woolley Marshall and the survivor of them and the heirs, executors and administrators respectively of such survivor, to defer calling in any money at the time of my decease lying in the hands of Messieurs Charrington and Company or of any other person or persons and also to defer the sale and conversion of all or any part of my real and personal Estate hereinbefore devised and bequeathed respectively in trust for sale and conversion and also all and any part of the hereditaments and premises which shall or may be purchased under the power hereinbefore contained for such time as to my said trustees or trustee, for the time being, may seem proper, without being answerable for any loss which may be occasioned thereby,

Provided always that it shall be lawful for the said John Nathan Bainbridge and Thomas Woolley Marshall and the survivor of them and the heirs, executors and administrators respectively of such survivor, to complete any building or buildings which at the time of my decease shall be in course of erection on any part of my real Estate and to defray the expence of such completion out of any portion of the said ["..." interlined] estate and if necessary to Mortgage or sell any part thereof for that purpose,

I give and devise all the freehold and Copyhold Estates which at my death shall be vested in me upon any trusts or by way of Mortgage and of which I shall at my death have power to dispose by Will unto the said John Nathan Bainbridge and Thomas Woolley Marshall and their heirs, Upon the Trusts and subject to the Equity of redemption, which at my death shall be subsisting or capable of taking effect therein respectively, but so that the money secured on such Mortgages be taken as part of my personal Estate,

And I hereby authorize and empower the acting Executors or Executor, for the time being, of this my Will to pay and satisfy all debts owing or claimed to be owing by or from me or my Estate and any liabilities to which I or my Estate may be subject, or may be alleged to be subject, upon any evidence they or he shall think proper and to accept any compositions or any security, real or personal, for any debt or debts owing to me or my Estate and to allow such time for the payment of any such debt or composition for a debt, either with or without taking security for the same, as to my said Executors shall seem reasonable and also to compromise and compound or submit to arbitration and settle all debts, accounts, transactions, matters and things which shall be owing, or claimed to be owing, from or to me or my estate or be depending or arise between me or my said Executors or Executor and any other person or persons and generally to act in relation to the premises in such manner as they or he shall think expedient, without being liable for any loss which may be occasioned thereby,

And I hereby declare that the receipt or receipts in writing of the said John Nathan Bainbridge and Thomas Woolley Marshall, or the survivor of them, or the heirs, executors or administrators of such survivor, or the trustees or trustee, for the time being, acting in the execution of the trusts of this my Will for the purchase money of any property hereby directed or authorized to be sold and for any other monies, stocks, funds or securities paid or transferred to them or him under or by virtue of this my Will, or in the execution of any of the trusts thereof, shall effectually discharge the person or persons paying or transferring such monies, stocks, funds or securities from the same and from being bound to see to the application, or being answerable for the misapplication or nonapplication thereof,

Provided always and I hereby declare my Will to be, that if the said Trustees hereby constituted, or any of them, or any trustee or trustees appointed as hereinafter provided, shall die, or be abroad, or desire to be discharged, or refuse or become incapable to act, then and in every such case it shall be lawful for the said Martha Caunt during her lifetime and after her death for the surviving or continuing trustees or trustee, for the time being and for this purpose refusing or retiring trustees shall if willing to act in the execution of this power be considered Trustees, or for the acting executors or administrators of the last surviving or continuing trustee, to appoint a new trustee or new trustees in the place of the Trustee or trustees so dying, or being abroad, or desiring to be discharged, or refusing or becoming incapable to act as aforesaid and that upon every such appointment all the estates, monies, stocks, funds and securities then vested in the trustees or trustee, for the time being, or in the heirs, executors or administrators of the last surviving or continuing trustee shall be so conveyed, assigned and transferred that the same may be vested in the surviving or continuing trustee or trustees jointly with such new trustee or trustees or in such new trustees solely as the case may require and that every trustee so appointed as aforesaid may, either before or after the said trust premises shall have been so vested as aforesaid, act or assist in the execution of the trusts and powers of this my Will as fully and effectually to all intents and purposes as if I had hereby constituted him a trustee,

Provided always and I hereby declare my Will to be, that the trustees or trustee, for the time being, of this my Will shall be respectively chargeable only for such monies as they shall respectively actually receive, notwithstanding their signing any receipt for the sake of conformity and shall be answerable and accountable only for their own acts, receipts, neglects and defaults respectively and not for those of each other, nor for any Banker, Broker or other person with whom any trust monies or securities may be deposited, nor for the insufficiency of any stocks, funds or securities not for any other loss, unless the same shall happen through their own wilful default respectively,

And also that it shall be lawful for the said trustees or trustee, for the time being, to reimburse themselves and himself or pay and discharge out of the said trust premises all expenses incurred in or about the execution of the trusts or powers of this my Will,

And lastly I revoke all former and other Wills by me at any time heretofore made,

In Witness whereof, I the said Benjamin Caunt have to this my last Will and Testament, contained in ten sheets of paper, to each of the first nine sheets and also at the end thereof set my hand, this twenty-fourth day of March in the year one thousand eight hundred and fifty three - Beng(ami)n [sic] Caunt - Signed, published and declared by the said Benjamin Caunt the Testator as and for his last Will and Testament in the presence of us, present at the same time, who in his presence at his request and in the presence of each other [sic] have subscribed our names as Witnesses thereto - Rich(ar)d Jones, Clerk to Mr Dangerfield, 26, Craven Street, Charing Cross - Mary Coaton, Searvent [sic] to Mr Caunt, Saint Martin's Lane.

On the 2nd day of October ["Le" struck through] Letters of Adm(inistrati)on with the Will annexed of the Personal Estate and Effects of Bengamin, otherwise Benjamin, Caunt, late of Saint Martin's Lane in the Parish of Saint Martin in the Fields in the County of Middlesex, Publican, deceased, who died on the 10th day of September 1861, at No. 90a Saint Martin's Lane aforesaid, were granted to Benjamin Butler Caunt the Son and, having attained the age of twenty one years, one of the Residuary Legatees substituted in the said Will, John Nathan Bainbridge and Thomas Woolley Marshall, the Executors and Residuary Legatees in Trust named in the said Will, having renounced the Probate and Execution thereof and also the Letters of Adm(inistrati)on with the same annexed of the personal Estate and Effect [sic] of the said deceased, Martha Caunt, the wife of the said deceased, the Residuary Legatee for life named in the said Will, having died in the lifetime of the said deceased."

BIBLIOGRAPHY

Bailey's Magazine of Sports and Pastimes, Volume 9, 1864
Bean, J.P., Bold as a Lion, 2002
Beardsmore, J.H, The History of Hucknall Torkard, 1909
Bell's Life in London, 1840 to 1870.
Brady, James, Strange Encounters, 1946
Brailsford, Dennis, Bareknuckles – A Social History of Prize-Fighting, 1988
Brampton, Baron, Reminiscences of Sir Henry Hawkins, Volume I and II, 1904
Butler, Frank, A History of Boxing in Britain, 1972
Chesney, Kellow, The Victorian Underworld, 1970
Cuming, E.D. (ed), Squire Osbaldeston: His Autobiography, 1926
Dowling, Vincent George, Fistiana, 1841
Egan, Pearce, Boxiana, 1812
Egan, Pearce, Book of Sports, 1832
Farnol, Jeffery, Epics of the Fancy, 1928
Gee, Tony, Up to Scratch, 1998
Golding, Louis, The Bare Knuckle Breed, 1952
Gorn, Elliot J., The Manly Art, 1986
Hartley, R.A., History & Bibliography of Boxing Books, 1990
Henning, Fred, Fights for the Championship, Volume 2, 1901
Johnson, Dick, Bare Fist Fighters of the 18th and 19th Century 1704-1861, 1987
Johnson Dick, The Bare-Knucklers, 1999
Lloyd, Alan, The Great Prize Fight, 1977
Mee, Bob, Bare Fists – The History of Bare-knuckle Prize-Fighting, 2001
Miles, Henry Downes, Pugilistica Volumes I, II and III, 1906
Sayers, Henry, Fights Forgotten, 1909
Sawyer, Tom, Noble Art, 1989
The Duke of Beaufort, K.G (ed), The Badminton Library of Sports and Pastimes, 1897
Wignall, Trevor, The Story of Boxing, 1923

INDEX

America, 17, 29, 48, 115, 116, 120, 123, 125
Angel, The, 31, 35
Appleby House, 23, 25
Barclay, Captain, 12, 13
Bell, The, 99
Bell's Life in London, 28, 31, 37, 149
Bendigo - see William Thompson
Bestwood Village Boxing Club, 7
Black Lion, The, 95, 96, 99
Boxiana, 12, 14, 210
Bradford, 27, 29, 49, 54, 57, 58, 60, 119
Brassey – see John Leechman
Broughton, Jack, 10, 11, 14, 15, 89, 90, 193, 194
Burke, James (Deaf 'Un), 29, 48, 51, 77, 80, 81, 128
Burn, Jem, 51, 61, 101, 103, 119, 127, 130
Butler, Ben, 23, 24, 26, 27, 31, 36, 65, 102, 127, 128, 130, 164, 166, 168, 169, 181, 184
Castle Tavern, The, 53, 57, 99, 114, 123, 126, 127, 128, 154
Cherry Tree, The, 99
Coach and Horses, The, 102, 119, 152, 154, 156, 159, 160, 161, 163, 164, 167, 168, 185, 186, 188
Corbett, James J., 10
Crawley, Peter, 53, 54, 58, 61, 62, 63, 71, 72, 77, 78, 82, 96, 97, 119, 127
Cribb, Tom, 58, 65, 115
Dowling, Frank, 19, 80
Dowling, Vincent, 13, 15, 18, 54, 63
Dutch Sam, 61, 78, 90, 93, 95, 99, 100

Egan, Pierce, 12, 13, 14, 210
Figg, James, 10, 14
Fistiana, 89, 91, 210
Freeman, Charles, 116, 118, 120, 121, 123, 125
Grear, 40
Greyhound, The, 96, 99, 168
Heenan, Tom, 17, 187
Hogarth, William, 13
Holt, Cicero, 86, 102, 103, 110, 112
Hucknall (Torkard), 7, 8, 20, 21, 23, 27, 31, 114, 187, 190, 192, 210
Kings Clere, The, 85
Lane, Hammer, 82, 85
Langan, Young, 29, 40, 49, 57, 58
Langham, Nat, 27, 163, 164, 166, 167, 168, 169, 172, 176, 180, 181, 183, 185, 187, 192
Lazarus, Izzy, 37, 120
Leechman, John (Brassey), 27, 29, 49, 50, 51, 52, 53, 54, 55, 57, 58, 60, 62, 63, 64, 65, 66, 67, 68, 69, 70, 71, 72, 74, 76, 77, 91, 96, 97, 102, 107, 112, 119, 131, 192
Liverpool, 27, 29, 31, 36, 48, 49, 52, 57, 77, 78, 80, 82, 96, 97, 99, 114, 115, 119, 127
Longford, Lord, 101
Looney, Bill, 27, 29
Mendoza, Daniel, 53
Miles, Henry Downes, 17, 210
Molineaux, Tom, 58
Molyneaux, Young - see James Wharton
New Rules, 14, 15, 88, 89, 90, 97
New York Spirit of the Times, 115

Nottingham, 7, 21, 23, 24, 25, 29, 31, 44, 45, 48, 51, 52, 57, 58, 60, 64, 96, 102, 119, 120, 126, 127, 128, 129, 130, 133, 134, 137, 139, 140, 145, 149, 151, 163, 172, 192
Nottingham Lambs, 44, 45, 137, 149, 163
Old Coach and Six, The, 114
Oliver, Tom, 60, 61, 101, 127, 128, 129, 171, 172
Osbaldeston, Squire George, 101, 130, 149, 150, 151, 210
Parker, Tass, 86, 119, 126
Pearce, Henry, 58, 210
Perry, William (The Tipton Slasher), 120, 121, 122, 125
Queen Victoria, 60, 61
Queensbury, Marquis of, 18
Salisbury, The, 188, 189
Salutation, The, 31
Sayers, Tom, 17, 164, 166, 167, 168, 169, 171, 172, 183, 187, 210
Sporting Life, 15
Spring, Tom, 47, 52, 53, 54, 57, 58, 61, 65, 78, 97, 100, 101, 102, 107, 114, 120, 123, 126, 127, 128, 129, 130, 132, 137, 141, 147, 148, 149
Star Hotel, The, 77
Sullivan, Yankee, 82
Sunrise Hill, 28, 192
Swan, The, 36, 37, 38, 48, 82, 127, 128
Taylor, George, 10

Taylor, Peter, 31, 36, 37, 41, 80, 82, 100
Thompson, William (Bendigo), 21, 23, 24, 25, 27, 28, 29, 31, 34, 36, 37, 38, 39, 40, 41, 42, 43, 44, 45, 46, 47, 48, 49, 51, 52, 55, 57, 58, 61, 77, 79, 80, 87, 91, 116, 119, 126, 127, 128, 129, 130, 131, 132, 133, 135, 137, 138, 139, 140, 143, 146, 147, 149, 150, 151, 163, 192
Times, The, 152, 158, 159, 185, 186
Tipton Slasher, The - see William Perry
Tom and Jerry, 14
Turner, Jem, 127, 130
Turner, Sam, 23, 24, 25
Ward, James (Jem), 29, 40, 48, 49, 58, 77, 78, 99, 113, 127, 128, 130, 143, 146
Ward, Nick, 37, 41, 51, 52, 77, 78, 79, 80, 82, 86, 96, 97, 100, 103, 104, 113, 128, 130, 135, 192
Wharton, James (Young Molyneaux), 31, 36, 41, 45, 47, 61, 62, 79, 82, 130, 137, 146
Whistling Oyster, 95
Whitaker, Joseph (Duke of Limbs), 21